TOUGH MARKET
NEW HOME SALES

By Jeff Shore

ISBN # 0-9801762-0-4

Printed by Signature Book Printing
Gaithersburg, MD

Cover design by Michele Tuggle (Michele@mprintstudios.com)
Edited by Elissa Weeks

Marketing Director: Cassandra Grauer (cassandra@jeffshore.com)

CONTENTS

Acknowledgements

Writing a book is, to understate, a daunting task. It takes time. It takes expertise. But mostly it takes guts. After all, what if nobody buys it? Or worse, what if nobody likes it? How would I live with myself if people didn't think my baby was beautiful?

And go figure – *Tough Market New Home Sales* is now in its fifth printing, and is consistently the #1 new home sales book on Amazon. com.

I am so grateful to those who daily encourage and inspire and who in some way have contributed to this work. Jason Forrest, Cassandra Grauer, the gang at Signature Books, Elissa Weeks, Michelle Tuggle, and so many others.

But most of all, thanks to all of you who made Deal With It! such a tremendous hit. Now in its fifth printing, I can't tell you what it means to hear the positive feedback and to know that, at least in this case, someone thought my baby was beautiful! Thanks so much.

How to Use This Book

This book was written in such a way that it gives you, the reader, intellectual flexibility. Feel free to read it cover to cover if you wish. If you do so, I strongly suggest that you use a highlighter, as I do when I am reading any skill improvement book. The point is that you should read actively, not passively. Read for implementation more than for edification. Knowing something new is good, but success comes through *doing* something new!

You can also use this as a reference book, turning to the chapter that addresses any specific concern you might have. For example, suppose that you've completed a sales presentation and you were bogged down on one particular point, perhaps dealing with the incentive question. Simply turn to that chapter, and focus on improving that one skill.

Next, you might consider quickly scanning the entire book and then going back and reading the sections or lessons that apply to you most urgently. No one said that you have to read this in order (go ahead – be a rebel!). I purposely have written the book so that each section is independent and can be seen as a separate lesson.

Further, you might consider reading this as a daily skill development book. Pick it up and read a couple of pages each day, focusing on one specific point of application. Then apply what you have learned when you are speaking with prospects. This is a great way to stay mentally sharp in the midst of a tough market.

Finally, many sales managers have reported that my last book, *Deal With It!*, made for great sales meeting discussions. My hope is that this book will provide similar opportunities.

Most importantly, no instructional book – not *Seven Habits*, not Biology 101, not even the Bible – has any relevance at all except that it changes insight and then behaviors. So I beg you not to simply read this book. I challenge you to find application points in every passage. My question for you is simple yet profound: What will you *do* differently as a result of what you read? Or to put it another way, where will you grow from here?

For Kevin, Emily, and Katie. I'll never be able to put into words how much I care for each of you. If I've never done anything else right in my lifetime, my children are a legacy of which I am immensely proud.

s.D.g.

Introduction

"Tut, tut, child," said the Duchess. "Everything has a moral, if only you can find it."
Lewis Carroll, *Alice in Wonderland*

This book was written on request. Hopefully it will soon be outdated.

I write from my office in Northern California, where the housing market has always been susceptible to enormous economic swings. In the past several years we've seen year-over-year-over-year appreciation that has exceeded 25% each year. And we've also seen $250,000 incentives on $800,000 homes. At the time of this publication, the latter of the scenarios is far more common.

Around the country homebuilders and sales counselors are singing a familiar refrain: five years (or ten in some markets) of incredibly strong growth ending in the harsh reality of salespeople scratching and clawing for every sale. Seemingly overnight, what was an incredible boom has become a spectacular bust.

And that's where it all gets a bit tricky. Have you ever heard this statement?

If you always do what you've always done,
you'll always get what you've always got.

Catchy, isn't it? Except that when it comes to the tough markets that inevitably follow strong markets, this statement is patently *Not True!!!!* If salespeople do in a tough market only that which they did in a strong market, they will get clobbered! In a very strong market sales counselors are absorbed by traffic management, price increases, huge backlogs, and sales by lottery. This creates a mindset in salespeople that the business will always come to them – what I call an "entitlement mentality."

In a tough market (or a normal market, for that matter) such a mindset will spell nothing but disaster and a quick exit from the industry.

Jennifer Cooper, Sales Counselor, Jacksonville, Florida

"When I first started in new home sales, we were selling nine or ten homes a month – it was great. I thought, 'This is wonderful – I can sell homes forever!'

"And then it was like someone just pulled the plug. We went two months without a sale. Our competitors started offering large incentives. We had a builder in our market offering a $100,000 incentive on a $275,000 home!

"I confess I was a bit shell-shocked. I was asking myself, 'What have I done? This career decision was a huge commitment. Have I bitten off more than I can chew?' At times it really got me down. The traffic was down, and cancellations were up. And the people who were coming through the door were suddenly in control."

So what are we left with? A whole lot of salespeople dealing with anything from justifiable discomfort to a major career crisis, wondering what it will take to turn the corner and survive the tough days. As I am traversing the country as a sales trainer and management consultant, I hear the stories. I see the looks in the faces. I can perceive that the market turn has crippled many who just a few short months ago were flying high.

And so this book was written at the request of salespeople who have either never seen a tough market or who have lived in a strong market for so long that they're struggling to make the adjustment to new realities.

Here is one such reality that you'd better get your hands around: truly great salespeople are market-proof. They are so well-rounded in their disciplines that they know how to thrive in any market! The fact is that there are thousands of people who purchase homes across the country each and every day. But the sales counselor who radiates positive energy and who practices proven and disciplined technique is the one who will inevitably land that sale.

Jennifer Cooper, Sales Counselor, Jacksonville, Florida

"Fortunately, I had great training from Tracy Miller, my VP of Sales. She really taught me confidence in myself and in my product. I really had to focus in on who those buyers were and what they really wanted. The customers just wanted to talk about incentives, but I needed to get them thinking about the true value of a beautiful new home. We had to take them by the hand and remind them of why they were making the purchase."

Look at it this way. In robust times it is more than sufficient for each salesperson to get his or her "fair share" of the market. After all, there is plenty of market to go around when sales are plentiful. But what if you only get "your fair share" in a tough market? That can only be equated with spectacular failure! Your fair share is not even close to what you need to survive the difficult markets. You need your fair share *and someone else's fair share!*

So may I recommend this mantra to you? Memorize it, and repeat it several times throughout the day:

All I want is more than my fair share.

Simple, isn't it? If my fair share of the smaller market isn't good enough, then all I want is *more* than my fair share.

Still, we can't stop there. It's not enough to *want* more than our fair share. The question is this: what do we need to do in order to *deserve* more than our fair share? You see, if I perform at the same level as the rest of the industry, I should expect my fair share. However, if I do things that others are not willing to do, if I go the extra mile and outperform my competition, don't I deserve more than my fair share? Of course I do!

Danny McElroy, Sales Counselor, Dallas, Texas

"It is easy to separate the good from the great when the market gets tough. The 'good' sales people have a slow down in sales pace because a large part of their success was market-driven; however, the 'great' remain consistent market-in and market-out. Evidence of this can be found by simply looking at the scoreboard, which in our business is the sales report."

My friends, I know of what I speak. I made a lot of money in a great market. *And then I learned how to sell in a tough market.* My sales manager at the time took our entire team through every aspect of the sales process; I learned from mentors who had been through it before; I read *New Home Sales* by the late Dave Stone, *Success in New Home Sales* by Richard Tiller, and anything else I could get my hands on. I embraced the opportunity to learn to be the best I could be.

The fact is that this market could lead you to an entirely new level of sales performance. And that will be entirely up to you. To paraphrase King Solomon, "There are lessons to be learned in times of adversity that cannot be learned in times of prosperity." There are growth opportunities in a tough market that can't be found elsewhere.

From that perspective, tough markets can be really and truly exciting! Who doesn't want to grow? You can go for a walk, or you can scale a mountain. You tell me where you'll find the best view!

A friend of mine put it this way: "Where will we grow from here?" I love that perspective. What will you be like on the *other* side of the challenging market? How you respond today will answer that question in advance.

> *"What is all knowledge, too, but recorded Experience?"*
> **Thomas Carlyle**

Are you up to the challenge? Because certainly it will be challenging. But for those who are committed to long-term success, the tough markets will make them truly great. It is true that if you choose to embrace the challenge, you'll have to go the extra mile in order to succeed, but as Zig Ziglar once said, "Go as far as you can see, and when you get there, you'll always be able to see farther."

My very best to you. May you rise to the occasion, face the task in front of you, and come out strong on the other side!

Jeff Shore
Auburn, California
November, 2007

TOUGH MARKET NEW HOME SALES

By Jeff Shore

Chapter One:
Getting Your Head On Straight

*"There comes a time in the affairs of man when he must
take the bull by the tail and face the situation."*
W.C. Fields, Comedian

"We will either find a way or make one."
Hannibal, Carthaginian General

Okay, so the market was red-hot, and we were all geniuses. Sales counselors were heroes and heroines. Sales managers were the definition of brilliance. Consultants were planning their own parades. Oh, sure, the market was strong, but it wasn't *that* strong. Much of the success came from our superior efforts, right? Right?

Even the home-buying customers played along. Many times the sales office conversation looked like this:

Sales Counselor:	*"Welcome to my community; here are the rules. Rule number one: no contingencies."*
Buyer:	*"Okay."*
Sales Counselor:	*"Rule number two: we don't cooperate with Realtors."*

1

Buyer:	*"Okay."*
Sales Counselor:	*"Rule number three: no investors."*
Buyer:	*"Ummm . . . Fine, I can lie about that one."*
Sales Counselor:	*"Rule number four: when I ask you to, you'll bring me a grande, extra-hot, one-pump mocha latte."*
Buyer:	*"With or without whipped cream?"*

All right, so maybe it wasn't quite that bad, but you have to admit that we had the upper hand. And I for one saw too many sales counselors take that for granted.

THE "ENTITLEMENT MENTALITY"

The problem in a prolonged healthy market lies in what I refer to as an "entitlement mentality" on the part of new home sales counselors. This mentality says, "If I show up for work and handle the rush of stuff that comes my way, I'll get my fair share of sales." It says, in a nutshell, "The market will come to me." We'll come back to this later.

And then the market suddenly changes. In the blink of an eye, we see the sub-prime mortgage programs evaporate. Dozens of non-contingent homebuyers suddenly "remember" that they are in fact contingent and now can't sell their homes. Investors and "quasi-investors" suddenly come up with creative excuses as to why they should get their deposits refunded. ("My company is downsizing, and I'm getting laid off, and I was so stressed that I went to the doctor, and he says I have a rare disease for which the cure costs exactly as much as my down payment. Oh, and I can't qualify anymore.")

Then there are those customers who are still in the market, but who now approach things with a much different and far more skeptical attitude. They generally fall into three categories:

1. The Angst Ridden: These prospects are so skittish that every

media report causes them to call Suicide Prevention. Facial tics are not uncommon; loud noises scare them.

2.   BWA's (Buyers with Attitudes): These are, ironically, the same people who agreed to all our rules in a hot market but who now walk through the door with a certain swagger, asking the question, "Who's your daddy, now?" (Gee, wherever did they learn such arrogance?)

3.   Psychotic-Amoral-Godless-Money-Sucker: You know, the incentive guy.

NOT TO MENTION THE MEDIA . . .

Always ready to pounce at the first sign of bad news ("If it bleeds, it leads!"), our friends in the media are joyfully hysterical that their now five-year-old prediction of a major market downturn is finally upon us. One writer starts things off, and everyone else piles on.

Here's a bit of flavor on that from the media. Check out these verbatim headlines and sub-heads from *USA Today*:

- "Mortgage Woes Shut Out Homebuyers"
- "Credit Panic Hits Nation's Largest Home Lender, Stocks, and Construction"
- "Mortgage Pinch Causes Domino Effect of Pain"
- "Home Sellers Stuck as Credit Crunch Shuts Out Buyers"
- "Housing Starts Plunge to '97 Levels"
- "Delinquencies, Foreclosures Expected to Rise"
- "Jumbo-loan Rates Jump"

How much is the media enjoying the downturn? What if I told you that every one of the above headlines appeared on *the same day in the same paper?* It's true, and it's proof positive that the media loves a good disaster. And if the reality is not as disastrous as they would like it to be, there's nothing they can't enhance with a little added melodrama!

Of course, the negative mentality isn't just limited to the homebuyers and the media. Realtors can be just as guilty of spreading gloom and doom. Homebuilding executives can send completely inappropriate messages about the market. Even many sales counselors have adopted a negative mindset that only confirms the fears of the homebuyers.

Tina Martelon, VP Sales, Denver

"In tough times you have to create your own cure. Your challenge shifts from managing transactions to simply managing your mental strength. You have to ensure that you don't become incapacitated by the looming negativity around you."

REDEFINING "THE MARKET"

"Worrying is like a rocking chair. It gives you something to do, but it doesn't get you anywhere."
English Proverb

"Pain is inevitable. Misery is a choice."
Anonymous

Something has to change, and I believe that the change toward a positive environment begins with top sales counselors in our industry. If we are not positive and optimistic, it's a good bet that our customers will follow our lead.

Let's start with our outlook on the market. The market is what the market is – deal with it! (Say, that would make a great book title.) We can discuss *ad nauseam* the state of the market, and it won't change a thing. You see, the factors that normally make up the housing market include the following: supply and demand, pricing, broad economic factors, competitive forces, job growth, interest rates, and mortgage availability. The problem with this list is that the factors it contains are all elements over which we have no control. This list suggests that we are victims of our circumstances. Moreover, it suggests that the customer is also such a victim!

But what if we just changed the definition of "the market"? What if we rewrote the definition so that it works on our behalf? After all, everyone is complaining that "the market" is bad. Why don't we change the definition of "the market" and make it good? I believe it is possible, using this very simple definition:

"THE MARKET" = 1 SALESPERSON + 1 HOMEBUYER

That's it. Yes, it's simple, but consider how profound this concept can be. I am that "1 Salesperson," and the next person who walks through the door is that "1 Homebuyer." If that person is in a position to buy, and I am in a position to sell, how strong is the market? IT'S PHENOMENAL! It is truly a GREAT market! The mindset of a top professional says, "Tens of thousands of people around the country will buy a home this week. Why not the guy who is about to walk into my sales office?"

How does this mindset affect the factors listed above? It renders them irrelevant! "The market" is no longer about interest rates, unless they affect this particular customer. "The market" is no longer about prices and incentives, unless they affect this customer's value equation.

We must come to grips with the idea that every customer who walks through the door brings his or her *own individualized market.* For example, do people sometimes buy in less-than-perfect locations? Of course they do; we've all sold our share of homes that are near highways or backing up to power lines. Sales in less-than-perfect locations demonstrate that those buyers represent "the market" for those particular homes.

A Lesson from a Customer

Some of us would *never* live in a home adjacent to a railroad track. But one sales counselor recently told me an anecdote in which she was showing a home next to a track when a train came by *during the demonstration.* The whistle blared as the train passed the sales counselor and her prospect. For a good two minutes they could say nothing over the noise and rumble of the train. The salesperson confided in me that she was horribly uncomfortable: "Those were the longest two minutes of my life. I couldn't wait until that train had passed so that I could move on to the next homesite." But as soon as the train was gone, the customer calmly stated, "Man, do I love that sound!" You see, that man was "the market." And how good was that "market"? It was great!

PERSPECTIVES FROM OTHER "TOUGH MARKETS"

Some valuable lessons concerning market perspective can be learned from studying markets that are not experiencing a significant downturn because there was no initial market swell. A good percentage of markets in the United States are seeing only modest effects from the broad national decline; the numbers year after year are fairly consistent. These markets did not see tremendous gains in the recent market boom. They are the "steady Eddies" of the industry.

One such market is Indianapolis, where both the prices and the sales pace have stayed fairly consistent over the past ten years. Sales counselors see perhaps five or, at the most, ten sales office visitors per week. For them, it is not at all uncommon to go for two or three days without having one new prospect come into the office. However, there is little anxiety about the potential for price increases because the prices do not adjust all that much over time.

As salespeople, how would we characterize the market in Indianapolis? If we take the broad view of the market, we would have to say that it is perennially soft. However, if we adopt the view that the market equals one homebuyer plus one salesperson, it is a GREAT market.

Alex Bashenow, Sales Counselor, Indianapolis, Indiana

"This business is not rocket science but is one of people science. If the person that you meet feels like they have been treated as if they matter, and the sales counselor has their best interest at heart, the customer is drawn into a purchase versus being pushed into a sale."

How does it affect our mindset when we have the perspective that the market equals one sales counselor plus one homebuyer? Consider these questions and their answers:

- How does it affect how we react to slower traffic levels? Theoretically, it means that a salesperson needs just three units of traffic to get three sales.

- How does it affect how we react to higher incentives from competitors? These incentives now only apply if the competitor has a more desirable home.

- How does it affect how we perceive "mean" people? We understand that mean people buy homes too, and they just don't buy them from weak-thinking salespeople.

- How does it affect how we perceive the practice of closing a buyer on his or her first visit to our community? If it's the right home, it doesn't make a difference which visit it is.

Here is the mindset that you *must* adopt: "The market" is walking through your door right now. The *entire* market is walking through your door right now. You get one shot with this particular market. Will you maximize the opportunity? It is only a matter of whether you will embrace the market or be a victim of it.

MAXIMIZING THE MARKET

> *"A pessimist sees the difficulty in every opportunity;*
> *an optimist sees the opportunity in every difficulty."*
> **Winston Churchill**

If entitlement is the mindset to avoid, what is the most advantageous mindset to adopt? The word to dwell on is this: *maximize!* You must maximize every sales office opportunity. This is the practice of top professionals. They maximize sales opportunities in these specific ways:

1. Top sellers maximize their opportunities to <u>sell</u> in a tough market.

Top professionals take advantage of every conversation and advance every sale as far as possible. Look at it this way. When a customer comes into a sales office and leaves without buying, it means that someone stopped the sale. Who did it? The prospect might stop the sale for legitimate reasons, but we must NEVER stop the sale. We must take every sale as far as it will possibly go.

2. Top sellers maximize their opportunities to <u>grow</u> in a tough market.

Allow me to be candid with you. I made a lot of money in a great market, but I learned how to be a salesperson in a tough market. As I said in the foreword, there are lessons to be learned in times of adversity that cannot be learned in times of prosperity. Are you willing to embrace those opportunities to learn and grow? You won't do that by default; you must have a plan. Current market conditions will provide you with an outstanding opportunity to grow in new and exciting ways if you commit yourself to that goal.

ENABLING THE "FUTURE GENIUSES"

In a tough market we find potential buyers sitting on the sidelines waiting for a rebound. But how will customers know when they have found the elusive "bottom of the market"? They only know this when they see it in the rear-view mirror! It will take a boldness on the part of the buyer to make a purchase decision in the face of negative inputs around them.

Our customers must recognize that the toughest of markets presents the greatest of buying opportunities. In fact, it is incumbent upon us as sales professionals to point out to our prospects that they are, in fact, future geniuses. It is true that these prospects will need to fly in the face of the nay-sayers if they choose to purchase when the market is challenging. But in the long run, people will look back at the wisdom and extraordinary foresight of their decision. All one needs to do is to consider previous real estate downturns. Everyone who purchases in a down market is eventually rewarded by a positive correction. They are the "future geniuses"!

SUMMARY

Think for a moment of the pressure you are putting on your prospect if you are not positive, upbeat, and energetic about the buying opportunity. Fear is rampant, to be sure. But what is the antidote to fear? What is the opposite of the fear? The opposite of fear is *confidence*. The good news here is that confidence is contagious! Thousands of people will purchase a home every week even in the toughest of markets. Do you really believe that they will choose to do this from a sales counselor who is infected with negative energy? I think not! They will seek out confident sales professionals, and they will adopt that confidence as their own.

Are the customers scared? Of course they are. But they are not so scared that they won't come through our doors. They are not so scared that they are sitting at home waiting for things to change. And if they are walking through the sales office door, they are carrying this message: "I'm thinking about this, despite what I read in the media, but I sure do need some help in this process. Are you confident enough for the both of us?"

THOUGHT-PROVOKERS

1. *What negative thoughts might you have about the market? Do you first need to "sell yourself" on the fact that this is a great buying opportunity?*

2. *If I asked you to tell me off the top of your head, with no pause or hesitation and with an abundance of energy, why this is such a good time to buy, could you do it? Does your argument provide confidence to potential buyers?*

3. *Might you be guilty of "stopping the sale" when the customer brings up a negative concern about the market? What mental disciplines would help you to take every sale as far as it will go?*

4. *What can you do to make sure you are positive, energetic, and confident in every single sales office conversation?*

Chapter Two:
The Remarkable Power
of Goal Clarity

Sales Manager:	*"So let's talk about your goals. What are you hoping to accomplish today? And remember my policy – be totally honest. Just tell me what you're actually planning."*
Salesperson:	*"Okay. In that case, I'm planning on a strategy of hope against hope that an all-cash buyer walks through my door in the next 30 minutes. Other than that, I plan to break my own Sudoku record of 3 minutes, 14 seconds on websudoku.com."*
Sales Manager:	*"Perhaps my 'be totally honest' policy needs some clarification."*
Salesperson:	*"And what are you hoping to accomplish today?"*
Sales Manager:	*"Spending time in the field as an excuse to hide from the boss."*
Salesperson:	*"Gotta hand it to you – that's totally honest!"*

In order to get the most out of our new perspective on the market, a solid commitment will be required on our part. Our attitude is not thrust upon us by the situations we face, unless we choose that path. To paraphrase Victor Frankl, we cannot control our circumstances, but we can always control our responses to our circumstances.

"Everything can be taken from a man but the last of the human freedoms –
to choose one's attitude in any given set of circumstances,
to choose one's own way."
Victor Frankl, Author, Psychologist, and Holocaust Survivor

With this premise in mind, I can think of no more important aspect of success in a tough market than a dedication to what I call strong goal clarity. Clear goals are critical to success in any market, to be certain, but challenging times have a way of sucking us into the negative atmosphere that surrounds the sales office. If we do not have a high degree of goal clarity in a tough market, we are likely to find ourselves unwittingly playing the role of victims.

Goal clarity gives us purpose and direction each and every day. It provides a positive counter-balance to the negative influences that so often take hold in a challenging market. Goal clarity focuses us. It reminds us that there is a bigger picture and that we have more control over our own success than we are often led to believe. Goals anchor us by providing a compass direction – we know where we are headed despite the blowing of the sales office winds.

In his outstanding book, *The Inner Game of Sales*, author Ron Willingham speaks of goal clarity as the single most important trait of a top sales professional. The Behavioral Sciences Institute in Dallas, Texas, which studies sales professionals around the world, lists "goal directedness" as one of two significant indicators of sales success (along with energy levels). In fact, we could fill page after page with information on the subject of goal orientation generated by some of the greatest sales thinkers of the last 100 years.

And yet, this remains something of a mystery to so many sales professionals. In my career I've met relatively few new home sales counselors who can show me their written goals or even describe their goals in abstract terms.

The challenging market might be giving you new motivation to re-think your approach on goal setting. If so, allow me to offer just a few pointers here. Bear in mind that this will be far from an exhaustive survey on the subject of goal setting. There is a lot of really great literature already out there; the world doesn't need my two cents on the subject. I will, however, endeavor to offer some suggestions on how you, as a new home sales professional, can get the most out of specific goal setting.

"I learned this, at least, by my experiment: that if one advances confidently in the direction of his dreams, and endeavors to live the life which he had imagined, he will meet with a success unexpected in common hours."
Henry David Thoreau, *Walden, or Life in the Woods*

"It's never too late to be who you might have been."
George Elliot, *The Big Goal*

If you spend any time studying the great John Wooden (*Wooden on Leadership* is an awesome read, by the way), you'll discover that the former UCLA basketball coach spent very little time talking about winning. Despite lining up the most impressive winning record in the history of sports, the man seems to have eschewed discussing the subject of which he was clearly the master.

Wooden knew that a person cannot always control outcomes; one can only control actions that lead to outcomes. His entire philosophy can be summed up into one simple yet profound phrase: *Play Perfect!*

This is all he ever wanted, from himself and from his team. Just play perfect, and everything else will fall into place. This simple philosophy can be applied in a myriad of ways. In the world of the new home sales, if I "play perfect," it means I . . .

- Show up with a high, positive energy every single day;

- Greet every prospect as the most important person on the planet;

- Carefully craft my sales presentation to maximize every opportunity;

- Take every sales conversation as far as it will possibly go;

- Take exceedingly good care of my backlog;

- Dedicate my best efforts to being an incredible teammate;

- Seek to improve my skills and performance every single day;

- Strive for excellence in all areas of my life.

Look over that list. Would you agree with me that the person who "plays perfect" in all those areas will find an abundance of success? Take a look once more. Are all the actions listed above in your realm of control? They are – and that's good news! You cannot always control the scoreboard, but you can always control your own efforts. You can always choose to *play perfect!* You can't always land a sale, but you can always do the things you need to do in order to land a sale.

Howard Flaschen, Sales Counselor, Jacksonville, Florida

"With a more challenging market, a site agent's faculties are certainly in the spotlight, and if ever there was a time to focus and be mentally prepared, this is it. I believe that one of the keys to being prepared is knowing your stuff and believing that you are the best site agent there is. Whether or not it is true is subjective, but the idea that you know that the person walking through your door hasn't received and will not receive better service than that which you can give them already puts you miles ahead of the competition."

DAILY GOALS

With "playing perfect" in mind, let's look at four specific activities on which you can focus each and every day to make goal-setting work for your career in new home sales. Select one to work on right away, and practice that goal until you are playing perfect. Top performers are activity-driven, and their activities complement their greater goals. If you don't see a goal on my list that gets you jazzed up, come up with your own. In fact, that goal might just be the most effective of them all.

1. Break sales goals into smaller activity goals.

For example, your goal might be to sell four homes at your community this month. Now, you cannot always control how many sales actually get written; you can only control your efforts toward that end. So break down the goal into the specific activities that will lead to the end result. Your list might look like this:

Goal: Four Sales
- Number of closing questions I must ask to get four sales: eight
- Number of people I need to take on site to ask eight closing questions: ten
- Number of people to whom I need to ask the Plan Close question: twenty
- Number of model demos I need to do to ask twenty Plan Close questions: thirty
- Number of traffic units I need to demonstrate thirty homes: forty

(I understand that these numbers are going to vary dramatically from market to market and that the above example might be WAY off for your area. Please go through this exercise and plug in the numbers that make sense for you.)

Now you can begin to track your specific efforts in each area. In other words, you can track whether you are *playing perfect* or not. Each week you can keep track not just of your traffic count but also of your model demonstration frequency, how often you ask the Plan Close question, how many site tours you give, etc.

Trust me – if you don't meet your sales goals, you'll find the variance in the numbers somewhere. And identifying the variance will give you a specific focus point for targeted performance improvement! This practice is no different from losing a basketball game and looking at the stat sheet: "Let's see, we shot well from the floor, and we made our free throws, but we turned the ball over twenty-five times that game, and the opponent scored thirty of their ninety points after our turnovers. Gentlemen, we're going to work on our ball control skills."

See how that works? You can see the power of goal-setting as you break the process down into specific activities. It is incredibly effective. Remember, you cannot always control the outcome, but you can *play perfect*!

2. Set a goal to change your circumstances.

Let's suppose that, after you analyze your efforts (see above), you realize that your traffic levels are insufficient to meet your activity goals. You have two options, both of which are under your control. First, you can improve your efficiency in other areas of the sale in order to increase your conversion rates. As you become more effective in the model demonstration, for example, you can lower the number of model demos you need to do in order to get to a Plan Close Question.

Your other option is to set a goal to change the circumstances, in this case to raise your initial traffic numbers. You only need to increase your traffic by a little bit if you increase your *quality* of traffic. The good news is that self-generated traffic is *always* of a higher quality than traffic generated by advertising, so you can absolutely expect to need a lesser amount of high-quality traffic in order to meet your goals.

If this is the situation in your community, please refer to Chapter Thirteen for a discussion on lead generation.

Danny McElroy, Sales Counselor, Dallas, Texas

"A big part of your positive attitude is to focus on constant personal development and improvement. Even if you are a consistent top producer, you can become complacent and assume that you already have everything mastered, which would be a huge mistake. When we stop learning, improving, and adapting to change we lose our edge and that's when "the market" beats us. I personally will always strive to keep that from happening to me."

---

3. Select a skill-development opportunity.

We can agree that output is a result of input, correct? And we can further agree that the higher the quality of the input is, the better the output will be, right? The difference between the London Philharmonic and the Warren G. Harding High School Concert Band is neither the music nor the instruments; it's the quality of the individual performances.

Think of your sales presentation as a concert in which you play every instrument. If your performance on any given instrument is weak, the concert will be less than optimal. When you nail down every part, you can expect success.

My observation in new home sales is that sales counselors are good at what they are good at and that they rely on those strengths to get them to a new contract. But what if they became proficient in all other areas as well? Wouldn't we expect the sales pace to rise dramatically?

So, with the goal of playing perfect in mind, why not find an "instrument" to work on and really focus on that for a day, a week, or a month? And I don't mean that you should practice until you can perform "Chopsticks." I mean that you should master the skill. This level of dedication is an outstanding example of goal setting in action.

As you look at the following list of skill-building practices, look for patterns more than for specifics. Apply the principles here to other areas of the presentation. Of course, if you need improvement in one of the areas listed below, by all means *go for it*!

- Ask ten questions in the first two minutes of the sales conversation. This action will serve to focus you on your understanding skills and will prevent you from information dumping right out of the gate. This is a great activity that has helped many sales counselors change their entire approach.

- Insert one powerful discovery question into your presentation three times daily. We're not talking about, "How many bedrooms?" or, "When were you thinking about moving?" The discovery questions that you should work on crafting are questions that the prospect will not hear in any other office and that will yield tremendous insight as to who your customers really are. Here are some examples: "Describe the perfect Saturday morning in your home." "When you go over to your best friend's house, is there something that you always look at and wish you had in your home?" "When you go for a walk, what are you hoping to experience?" When you ask these types of questions, you will learn volumes about the character of your customer and will stand apart from every other salesperson.

- Practice the handling of a tough objection, such as incentives. At the start of the day, picture a sales conversation where someone asks you about incentives right off the bat. Practice what you will say to diffuse and defer that conversation (Yes, practice it out loud!). When a customer does ask the question, try to stay with your script as best you can; then, when the customer leaves, evaluate your performance and prepare for the next encounter. With this or any other objection, commit to practicing your response in advance.

- Ask the "Plan Close" question to five of your next ten sales office visitors. This aim is just one of what could be 100 specific benchmark goals, but the idea here is to find one specific target in the sales presentation and work toward it. When you have this goal in mind, it will affect your entire presentation because you will know that your conversation must lead to this one point.

- Site 50% of your traffic. For some, the number will need to be higher, for some, lower. The point is that you should have a goal in mind (and track it!) that dictates your entire presentation. If you know that you're going to site a specific percentage of your traffic, you will find that you are far less likely to stop the sale, that you will take every conversation as far as it will go.

- Hit 100% phone follow-up within twenty-four hours with every visitor this week. The key in this goal is that it is specific; there is no grey area on this. You either did it, or you didn't, so you have immediate feedback on whether you played perfect or not.

What's great about this list is that it is 100% track-able. You can hold yourself accountable because you know quite clearly whether you accomplished your goals or not. Goal clarity works that way; it provides a target toward which you can track your progress.

Thang Nguyen, Sales Manager, San Ramon, California

"A truly unique sales associate can be a huge difference maker and revenue generator. The top 3% of any sales organization obviously have great sales technique, ability to garner trust, ambition, motivation and compas-

> *sion. But even more, it is these individuals, already in the top 3%, who continually find a motivation to improve. These superstar professionals realize that success and failure are less dependent on market conditions, and more the embodiment of the control and will that you can exert upon any customer in any sales interaction."*

4. Set a service-oriented goal.

A service-oriented goal doesn't have to be specifically related to sales skills. Since customer care is such a high priority in the life of a new home sales counselor, a goal involving customer care will go a long way toward both improving your sales performance and motivating you to provide outstanding service. Moreover, when you focus in on this area, you will find that the positive energy it fosters will spill over into your conversations with new prospects. The following are suggestions for customer care goals:

- Return buyer phone calls within sixty minutes whenever possible. You'll surprise people with your immediate attention.

- Begin the calls to your backlog with a sales-oriented message. Remind customers of why they purchased in the first place, and provide them with additional confidence that they've done a very good thing. This will work to counteract all the negative input they receive when they purchase a home in a tough market.

- Provide custom-tailored community information to both prospects and to your buyers in backlog. For instance, if they have children, get them the contact information for the local youth soccer league and a list of all the parks in the area, not just the closest one.

- Have a cookie-baking day and make dozens of cookies. Drop them off at your customers' homes with a note that says you care. This is especially effective around a holiday.

- Pay four teenagers ten dollars an hour and have a car wash morning for all your prospects and buyers. Tell them to stop by between ten and twelve on Saturday for a free car wash and refreshments. An investment of $100 will pay big returns.

- Brainstorm customer care. At your next sales meeting, challenge your peers to come up with unique ideas on how to go the extra mile for the customers.

One more thing about goal clarity – it restores your sanity. Your circumstances might bring you all kinds of anguish on any given day, but your goals say that there is at least one aspect of your professional life over which you have complete control. You can lock the door at the end of the day knowing that you were in control of this one important area of your professional life. Without a goal, you are left to be the victim of your circumstances, and that mindset is completely inconsistent with that of a top performer.

THE MENTAL APPROACH TO THE DAY

"Every day begins with possibilities. It's up to us to fill it with the things that move us towards progress and peace."
Ronald Reagan

"This is the day that the Lord has made. We will rejoice and be glad in it."
Psalm 118:24

In a strong market there is little need to get "psyched up" to face the day. The mentality is more like, "fasten your seatbelt – it's going to be a wild ride." So for those sales professionals that endure a major market shift, they must also consider the major mental shift in regards to their daily mindset. A gloom-and-doom, woe-is-me attitude is a sure-fire recipe for disaster, and it will spell a quick end to your new home sales career.

We talked in Chapter One about "getting your head on straight," so now let's put some very specific ideas in place that will help you to begin your day in control. That is the goal – to control what you can control, and you can control your own mental approach. The key here is that you must turn your personal desire for excellence into specific action. In other words, you cannot simply read these words and make a decision to have a better attitude in regards to how you face the day. That decision must be followed by action.

Howard Flaschen, Sales Counselor, Jacksonville, Florida

"This market is certainly an energy sucker and it can make one want to stay in bed. The thing that I use to help stay on top and pump up my own energy is self-belief. I'm a firm believer that self-confidence is the personal foundation that you have to start with. If you are nervous before a buyer shows up because you don't feel confident in what you know and who you are, than you're already putting yourself at a disadvantage to your competition. It is the selling to yourself that you are the best in the business that will help you help the buyer and get them into what is right for them."

It has been said, and appropriately so, that excellence is a habit. And the most powerful habit that I can think of for a new home sales counselor is to start the day confident and in control. Far too many sales professionals sleepwalk through the early part of the day. Their drive to the sales office is spent listening to Howard Stern or random radio stations. They get to the sales office, unlock the models, and wait for the business to come to them. And they struggle – mightily.

I have a coffee almost every morning; it wakes me up. I have something to eat every morning; it's good for me, and it gets my body fueled up. Many of you have the same experience each and every day, and when you don't get your coffee . . . watch out world! When we don't get our beloved cup of coffee, we lose our edge. We are cranky and short-tempered. WE NEED OUR COFFEE! Think of the irony. We wouldn't dream of starting the day without our coffee, but we think nothing of starting the day without *waking up the brain*! We'll go through the routine of work without any jolt, without any focus. We do things to wake up our body; what do we do to wake up our spirit????

You must start every day with a commitment – a daily goal that focuses you on excellence. You must make the decision to start the day strong and in control of your mental state. Otherwise, you will by default make a decision to start the day with others in control. That's right – any time you don't start the day in control, you give the control over to others. You will be nothing but a victim of your circumstances.

Here are some specific ideas for starting the day strong and in control:

1. Visualize the perfect sale.

This is going to sound crazy, but I once sold a home to an invisible prospect while driving in my car. It's true. I was on a seven-hour drive from Southern California to Northern California after dropping off my son Kevin for his sophomore year of college. I was listening to a CD on sales skills, and it got me juiced up about selling a home. So I sold a home - out loud - to an imaginary buyer in the seat next to me.

What's crazier still is that by the time I got the sale (and not to brag, but this was a tough buyer with some really difficult objections!), I was fired up. At that moment I had a really strong desire to actually sell a home.

When we visualize the perfect sale, we get our minds into the "selling mood." That is, we are mentally prepared to have that sales fantasy come to life. So, why not take some time in the early part of the day to visualize playing perfect? Picture a willing and qualified prospect in the early part of the conversation. Walk him or her through a model, and look for a positive reception of your value points. Throw out a tough objection, and handle it with ease. Then go for the close, and imagine the joy of both you and your prospect when you get a "yes."

Sound crazy? Is it any crazier than sleep-walking through your morning routine and expecting you'll be in a selling frame of mind by default?

2. Choose a sales technique to work on throughout the day.

If you start your day with a commitment to work on one specific skill in every conversation with every prospect, you accomplish two powerful things. First, you are committing in advance to *playing perfect*. Second, you are getting yourself into the selling mindset right from the start. The goal clarity associated with that one specific area will pay huge dividends, both in your skill set and in your mindset.

Here are some final principles for selling in a tough market that you can practice every day:

- Offer one piece of encouragement to a co-worker every day. He or she will feel great, and *you* will feel great! What an awesome way to start the day!

- Commit to one ABCD ("Above and Beyond the Call of Duty") act of service for a customer every day, and plan it out in advance. In a tough market everyone is susceptible to negative emotions, including your buyers. To give them the reassurance that they need, commit early in the day to go above and beyond to help them with a need. Find a specific way to help a specific customer in an extraordinary way. Think about the impact you'll create if you do this every day. Even if nothing else goes right all day long, you'll be able to say that you did something worthwhile.

- Grow – somehow – every day. This is the surest way to protect your own sanity. Use the tough-market time to get strong; use the time to develop your knowledge. Take advantage of the selling floor as a practice laboratory.

Before you move on to some of the nuts and bolts of the sales process in a tough market outlined in this book, will you consider really getting your hands around your mental approach? My friend, if you don't have this part right, nothing else will matter. You can technique your customers to death, but if your heart is not in the right place, you will join the roster as yet another manipulative salesperson. Take pride in what you do, and get it right between the ears. Everything else will follow.

> *"A man can succeed at almost anything for which he has unlimited enthusiasm."*
> **Charles Schwab**

SUMMARY

Everyone is looking for an edge in a tough market. Focusing on your goals might be just the advantage you need to stay sharp, to protect your sanity, and to get more sales! But this doesn't happen by commitment. It doesn't happen by decision. It happens by action! If you are truly committed to effectively using the power of goals, you must take action right away. Don't read on until you have this part down solid!

THOUGHT-PROVOKERS

1. *Have you ever had success in setting and reaching goals? If so, go back to that mindset and relive how you felt and acted. Remember the victory of when you accomplished your goal and the energy boost that came with it.*

2. *There are plenty of great books on the subject of goal setting. Read one this week. Start with Brian Tracy's book <u>Goals!</u>. It's simple, straight-forward, and motivating.*

3. *Do you know someone who can help you in this area? Find a goal accountability partner and challenge one another to accomplish big things.*

4. *Are your goals in writing? There is no question – if it is not written down, it has a fraction of the potential for success. Take some time and write those goals down – today!*

Chapter Three:
The Critical Twelve Seconds

Salesperson:	*"Welcome to..."*
Customer:	*"What are your incentives?"*
Salesperson:	*"Wait – I'm supposed to make a good first impression before I answer that question."*
Customer:	*"Huge incentives make a good impression. How much are they?"*
Salesperson:	*"Can I interest you in some rapport-building repartee before we talk about incentives? I read in a book that I should do that first."*
Customer:	*"And I read in the last sales office that you guys are desperate."*
Salesperson:	*"Oh, since you put it that way, we're at $50,000."*
Customer:	*"I was looking for at least $100,000. I'm outta here."*
Salesperson:	*"Here's my card. Call me if you want to bond."*

Step into the shoes of a homebuyer on a search for the perfect home in the perfect community. When customers approach the new home sales office, what are they thinking? Here are some of the thoughts that are likely rushing through their minds:

- "What will the salesperson be like?"

- "Should I be afraid?"

- "I've heard it's a tough market."

- "Don't forget to ask about incentives."

- "Don't let that salesperson control or manipulate."

- "Was my cousin Ralph correct when he said it was a lousy time to buy?"

- "I must not show how much I like the home."

- "This is really scary."

Many salespeople fail to see the world through the eyes of their customers. Top performers not only consider the customers' stresses and concerns, but also adopt their paradigm and understand their mindset. It's the difference between sympathy and empathy, between feeling sorry for a person and actually feeling what a person feels.

A top performer in a tough market will recognize the customer's burden of both past experiences and negative perceptions. The customer not only has less experience with home sales than a salesperson, but often has bad sales experiences along the way. Customers make assumptions about salespeople based on relatively limited encounters. For example, a customer's entire knowledge of salespeople may be comprised of a past condo purchase that didn't go well, a time share presentation that was particularly abrasive, the last new home community they visited, or having rented the movie "Glengarry Glen Ross," which depicts Realtors in a less than glamorous light. They are working with limited knowledge and a wealth of assumptions.

Now let's throw on top of that the homebuying stresses associated with a challenging market. A top performer will understand how market conditions tend to elevate the customer's fear level. The buyer will question the wisdom of the decision, his or her own understanding of the situation, and the opinions of other people. Buying a home is a stressful decision in *any* market. When a tough market is added to the mix, it becomes truly anxiety-laden.

Successful sales counselors will assume the customer's desperate need for respect and attention in times of stress. The best of the best understand how critical it is to *start strong* and to use this one-and-only chance to make a great first impression. Top performers understand their critical role in alleviating buyers' fears right out of the gate.

> *"Energy is beauty. A Ferrari with an empty tank doesn't run."*
> **Elsa Peretti**

MANAGING THE ENERGY LEVEL

Consider what I believe to be the single greatest difference between a successful new home community and a neighborhood that is seriously struggling. In fact, it's the same phenomenon that distinguishes a strong market from a challenging market. What is this critical success factor? In a word: *momentum*! Show me a community with huge momentum, and I'll show you success.

Customers are impressed by sales momentum. They find comfort in its presence. Momentum equals positive energy, and customers need to see this energy as an indicator that others have gone before them and, in so doing, have created a safe environment. In short, no one wants to buy where no one else wants to buy.

Of course, we cannot fake success; we cannot show momentum where it does not exist . . . or can we? What if we could define the "look" of momentum? We can – it's called energy. High-energy environments look successful. This is true in new home sales offices, restaurants, shopping malls, cocktail parties, grocery stores, and anywhere else where people relate to their environmental surroundings. High positive energy is critical in showing success.

Jim Suth, Sales Trainer, Danville, California

"Alright, this is going to sound crazy, but you need to keep yourself in the game. You need to write notes to yourself and put them on the mirror. Use post it notes. Pretty colors are the best. Stop laughing!! When I got up in the morning and read that note that said "Hey Sexy! Go get em!", of course I recognized my own writing, but that didn't stop me from going to work laughing and feeling good. It was going along fine until my wife figured out my game. One morning the note said "Hey good looking, do the dishes!". I knew I didn't write that one. It didn't wreck my day though. I just needed to hide my motivational gems somewhere else!"

Take, for example, the restaurant industry. When you enter the Cheesecake Factory on a Friday night at seven o'clock, you can immediately sense the energy. Diners fill every seat, servers are whizzing past, and the place is echoing with excited voices. The energy is palpable. This energy means popularity, and popularity is associated with quality. Even though they may have to wait, diners choose the Cheesecake Factory over, say, an empty Chinese restaurant, not necessarily because of the food, but because of the high positive energy in one place and the low energy in the other.

Consider similar energy experiences in Best Buy, Car Max, Disneyland, or (if you're lucky enough to live on the West Coast) In-N-Out Burger. All build the customer experience around energy, and this energy breeds momentum.

It doesn't take customers long to determine the energy level when they enter a new home sales office. In fact, this energy assessment takes just a few seconds. They sense it in the lighting, the music (if any), the displays, and the perceived busyness.

But more than anything, they sense the energy in the salesperson. Here's one example: A couple of years ago I entered a new home sales office in San Antonio, Texas. I was not immediately greeted, and it made me feel a little uncomfortable. After several moments a woman came out from behind her desk to greet me. As she did so, I noticed she was carrying a Danielle Steele novel . . . *with her finger marking the page she was reading at the time.* What are the messages she was sending to me? One, "You're interrupting me." Two, "I'd like to get back to the novel, so please make this quick." Three, "There's nothing going on here. I have plenty of time to read this book." How much energy was in that sales office? NONE!

Of course, the violations don't have to be nearly that egregious in order to destroy the energy in the sales office. Leave the customer standing alone for a few seconds upon entering the office, and the energy is immediately drained. Lean against the doorway or on the topo table, and you'll display low energy. It only takes the customer a few moments to read the energy level in a new home sales office. These moments are critical, requiring the salesperson to be one-hundred-percent "on" for every buyer who walks through the door.

This discussion is particularly important in a tough market. Customers are hyper-sensitive and ultra-anxious. They need immediate energy assurances from a fully engaged salesperson. Consider the incredibly fast trigger-finger of a customer who faces too much choice and needs to make a quick decision on whether they will eliminate your community from contention. That decision could be made simply by gauging the feel of the sales office based upon the interaction with the sales counselor.

> *"Energy, not time, is the fundamental currency of high performance.*
> *Performance, health and happiness are grounded*
> *in the skillful management of energy."*
> **Jim Loehr & Tony Schwartz, The Power of Full Engagement**

THE CRITICAL TWELVE SECONDS

Critical moments exist throughout the sales process; however, none are more critical than the first twelve seconds. *Together, the five seconds before the customer walks through the door of the sales office and the seven seconds immediately thereafter decide the fate of the sale.* It is a do-or-die experience in the sales process.

The sale is in peril during the first twelve seconds for many reasons. First of all, research shows that people determine whether they like someone or not within seven seconds of meeting him or her for the first time. We all do this on a subconscious level when we meet someone new. We size up his or her energy and character, and after seven seconds we make that decision: do I like this person?

Likeability is established within seven seconds, and likeability is the earliest foundation of trust. As a salesperson, being immediately likeable will work to preserve the sale and will leverage your pre-shot routine (we will discuss this shortly).

The key here is to decide *before* the customer even enters the office that you will be likeable and then to act on this decision. Remember, being likeable is a conscious and unilateral act.

This principle holds true in any market, but in a tough market it is especially salient. In a strong market, the buyer needs the salesperson, and so the salesperson can exist without likeability. In a tough market, the likeability factor can be a deal-killer. The customer is looking for elimination opportunities, and one of these eliminating factors is an unlikable salesperson. Many customers comment on the fact that they would never buy a new home because of their experience with a salesperson they just didn't like very much.

Fortunately, the converse of this is also true. Customers will continue to buy new homes because of great salespeople, and great salespeople earn that reputation by coming through during critical moments, especially when times are tough. They recognize that making a first impression is a critical moment, and they seize the opportunity to earn the trust of their customers.

> *"We are happiest when we are making the greatest contribution."*
> **Robert Kennedy**

> *"Happiness is a perfume which you cannot pour on someone without getting some on yourself."*
> **Ralph Waldo Emerson**

THE HALO EFFECT

The up-side of likeability is that after a person establishes that early rapport, it is difficult to destroy it. Psychologists call this "the halo effect." This principle says, "If I like you after seven seconds, I will continue to like you thereafter." Of course, the converse is also true. "If I dislike you after seven seconds, I will continue to dislike you thereafter." So the early efforts towards likeability will pay huge dividends as the sale progresses.

THE PRE-SHOT ROUTINE

Watch Tiger Woods before he takes a shot; watch him size up his environment and assess the situation. Mostly, look for signs of his mental focus as he prepares for the swing. He is visualizing the perfect swing and the perfect result. Golfers refer to this process as the "pre-shot routine," and it is critically important to their success.

Top performers are ready to be liked even *before* the customer walks through the door. They have developed their own "pre-shot routine," and it could be the single most important step a salesperson can take in the sales office. The pre-shot routine is about mentally preparing oneself for the sale before the customer opens the door of the office. It is being mentally "on" and one-hundred-percent engaged, in a strong position to serve and to sell. Getting this right will set the tone for the entire transaction.

Bear in mind that in a strong market the energy of the marketplace will boost you up and allow you to be carried by market momentum. In a challenging market it is up to you to provide that energetic lift. You can do this through conscious effort directed toward high positive energy.

Here are some tips for establishing a "pre-shot routine":

1. Make a decision that the customer is here to purchase. Say to yourself, "Hundreds of people will buy a home in this market this week – why not this person?"

2. Take a deep breath. It serves to disconnect your mind from all your past activities and focus you on the task at hand.

3. Smile *before* the customer comes through the door. People like to see people who smile all the time, not just when they have to.

4. Commit to remembering the customer's name. Ninety percent of memory technique is based on concentration, so make this your goal from the start. This is a tremendous advantage in a challenging market because it allows you to more easily stand apart from your competitors in a very personal way. Learn it and use it!

5. Plan out your opening statement. The time to come up with your opening statement is *not* when your customer is standing in front of you. Be strategic!

6. Say something out loud that fires you up: "Showtime!" "I am on!" "Time to sell a home." "I have seven seconds to be liked." Say it out loud (assuming that there is no one else in the office!). The very action will help you focus.

Above all, commit to a pattern that seems comfortable to you, and then work on it.

Robert Morganti, VP Sales, Las Vegas, Nevada

"One thing that I found to be extremely effective in these down times is positive thinking. If we as managers believe that the market is down and that we expect sales are going to be low, our sales professionals start to believe it as well. Positive thinking is a key attribute of a leader, and people follow good leaders. I heard it put this way: "Show me a leader with no followers and I'll show you a guy out on a walk!"

Making a strong mental effort to utilize the five seconds before the customer enters the office might be the single-most important thing you can do to boost your success in a tough market. If you don't yet have a specific "pre-shot routine," put this at the top of your action list!

THE FIRST SEVEN SECONDS

After the customer has entered the office, the first seven seconds of conversation with the salesperson are critical. As the salesperson, you should be conscious of body language, facial posture, and positioning. But more than anything, you must be aware of your need to connect with a customer who is going through a stressful time and truly needs your help.

Here are a few ideas for maximizing the first seven seconds:

1. Be on the move. Movement is energy, and it is imperative that you show high energy. If you are moving toward the customer, it follows that you are moving *from* some other activity. And this implies that there is something going on in the office, namely sales!

The next time you're at the mall, stop in at a Gap store. You'll notice that the employees are always on the move. That's by design. The leadership team knows that movement equals the perception of energy and momentum, and that customers gravitate to these organizational characteristics. No one wants to buy where no else wants to buy, so customers follow the energy. This principle certainly holds true in a new home sales office.

2. Practice good facial posture. The very term "body language" is a misnomer. Ninety percent of effective body language takes place from the neck up. People talk a lot about good posture, but the way to excellent body language is through strong *facial* posture. Think of lifting your face and showing strong energy with your eyes. Having a mirror in your office helps as well – you can do a quick check-up before someone comes through the door ("Do I look happy to be here?").

3. Show gratitude before anything else. Let your customer know that you appreciate the visit right from the start: "You had a lot of choices for where you could have stopped, but you came here. Thank you so much." Just a brief statement of gratitude shows prospects that they are appreciated, and this is a message that you can both enforce and leverage throughout the conversation.

As a consultant, I watch mystery shop tapes all the time, and it is amusing to try to spot the moment in the tape when the salesperson realizes that he is being shopped. Suddenly, the energy level increases dramatically; the salesperson becomes strong and motivated. This is wrong on many levels. The encounter should have been high-energy from the start! What was the salesperson waiting for? He was probably looking for the coveted "buying signal" from the prospect. I'm a contrarian on this point. I believe that buying signals are overrated;

only mediocre salespeople wait for customers to demonstrate their passion before becoming willing to take them seriously.

To my mind there is only one legitimate buying signal, and that is when the prospect comes through the door. Anything less than full engagement is a sign of an entitlement attitude, of a salesperson who thinks, "If I just show up for work, people will come into my office and let me know that they're interested." I suppose this could work in a red-hot market, but in a challenging market such thinking will get you creamed!

Gary Hendrickson, Hendrickson Marketing, Tacoma, Washington

"A tough market or a good market is more about your mental approach then anything else. Jeff once told me about how he rather enjoyed dealing with mean buyers, trying to get them turned around. After all, they are still buying homes, and they buy from people they like and trust. Enthusiasm and attitude – that's the key."

THE OPENING STATEMENT

Here you're probably hoping that I will give you "the mother of all opening lines," perfect for use in a tough market. Sorry to disappoint, but I cannot do that. The opening statement must be a reflection of the sales counselor and the early "vibe" that is immediately established with a customer.

I can only offer a rule of thumb: Your opening statement should complement your overall objective. If you want to build a relationship with the customer, I suggest a relationship-building statement. Too many salespeople fall into ruts by using the same questions over and over again, and all too often these questions weren't that effective in the first place. Here are some examples of less-than-effective opening statements:

- "Can I help you?" A valid interpretation of this question is, "You go first. If you can come up with some intelligent questions, I'll counter with some intelligent answers." The problem with this opening question is that it ensures that you, the salesperson, are out of control from the very beginning of the encounter. Furthermore, it pressures customers to perform, and they often handle this pressure with two unfavorable responses. "I'm just looking," or "What are your incentives?" With either reply, you have begun the conversation in a hole.

- "What brought you in here today?" When I hear this question in the sales office, I wonder if the salesperson isn't really saying something like, "I'm hoping you're a lay-down, who will respond to my question by saying, 'I'm here to buy a home. Would you please sell me one?'" First of all, the customer is never going to say this, but even further, there is no reason for you to ask this question. You should begin by assuming that the customer has come into your office to buy a home. If you ask a question like this, you shouldn't be surprised when a wise guy responds with, "We caught a ride on the Orient Express. What do you think brought us here? We drove!"

- "How did you find us today?" The customer's interpretation of this question is, "It is more important to me that I make the marketing department happy than it is to start a functioning relationship with my customer." Truthfully, this question is not even relevant to initiating the sales process. It's important information to obtain, but to open the conversation with this question is a waste of the first-impression opportunity.

- "Is this your first time here?" The customer can interpret this question as, "Let's dispense with that whole relationship thing and get right into the sales presentation, shall we?" Instead of this approach, try communicating to the customer this message: "You're a real person, and I'm a real person, so why don't we forget our roles as 'salesperson' and 'prospect' for just a moment and connect as real people?"

These less-than-adequate opening questions are evidence of a poorly conceived sales process. Top performers take care never to put their customers in the position of having to control the early conversation. Top performers are willing and eager to take the leadership role in the sales encounter.

> *"Make a habit of dominating the listening and let the customer dominate the talking."*
> **Brian Tracy**

SUMMARY

In the end, the actual opening statement or question is not as important as attitude, motivation, and heart. A dedicated salesperson is engaged and ready to build a trust-based relationship with his or her customer. Eventually this engaged attitude will benefit both the customer and the salesperson. Remember, in a tough market, the salesperson has to take the lead. In this sales climate, a weak opening can kill a career in a hurry.

While this conversation starts with the mindset and then the strategy, it is the action that makes the difference. Don't leave this subject without some clear ideas on action steps you can take to maximize your effectiveness in this area of your presentation.

THOUGHT-PROVOKERS

1. *What do your customers see when they walk into your sales office? Do they see high energy? Do they see likeability? Do they see momentum?*

2. *Have you established a specific "pre-shot routine"? What can you do in those five seconds before the customers come into the sales office to make sure you are 100% engaged?*

3. *Do you really believe (REALLY BELIEVE!) that the customer is here today to purchase a home? Or are you waiting for buying signals to see if you have a "hot prospect"?*

4. *Do you need to change up your opening statement or question? What would work more effectively for you?*

Chapter Four:
Strategic Discovery

Sales Manager:	*"So Barbara, tell me what you discovered about that last prospect."*
Salesperson:	*"Well, she wants four bedrooms and three baths, around 2,000 square feet, single-story on a ¼-acre homesite."*
Sales Manager:	*"That's great. But what did you learn about her personally?"*
Salesperson:	*"Oh, that. She is frustrated with her husband's general lack of affection and unwillingness to help around the house. Part of that might be based on some deep-rooted insecurity based on a largely absent father. She plays Bunko on Tuesdays but thinks that her friend Margaret cheats and her friend Joanne has horrible breath. Oh, and she has this growth on her..."*
Sales Manager:	*"That might be too much discovery on your part."*
Salesperson:	*"So, you're saying you don't want to hear about the growth?"*

"Outspoken! Me? By whom?!"
Dorothy Parker

In a strong market, the sales process is almost surreal. The conversation is heavily lop-sided; the salesperson does the talking and makes the decisions while the customer just goes with the flow. Sales counselors can seemingly do no wrong. They are in a zone, and they are in control. In fact, when a market is white-hot, customers might purchase homes that do not truly meet their needs just so they do not get left behind. In these cases, sales counselors can sell a home to a customer without really understanding that customer's needs, wants, and desires.

In tough markets, salespeople have a new demand placed on them – they must truly and deeply understand their individual customers. In this more challenging environment, sales professionals cannot get away with making assumptions; they must really get to know and understand the prospect, and they must do so quickly. In a tough market, customers have less patience; their fears affect many aspects of the sale, including their own attention spans.

Most salespeople simply do not question in a strategic way. They have not sat down and planned the questions that they intend to ask during the sales presentation. If they did, the same questions wouldn't come up in every sales conversation. These "same" questions tend to be checklist-type questions that cover bedroom count, price range, qualification ability, and so on. The answers to these questions are important to know, but if salespeople stop here, they are ill-equipped to advance the sale because they do not have a deep understanding of their prospects.

Tammy Blount, VP, Mystery Shopping Company, Seattle, Washington

"If there is one thing I would encourage sales professionals to do, it would be to take control by understanding the buyer. Seize the opportunity to stand out from the competition by asking probing questions. Be curious. Find out what is important to THEM, and use your arsenal of value and

> *benefits to tie them emotionally to both you and your homes. Don't worry about what ABC Builder down the street is giving away – give your customer what they are looking for through THEIR eyes, and they'll be buying YOUR home."*

The problem with this kind of "just-the-facts" approach is that these questions don't yield particularly productive answers. They are typically close-ended questions that generate one-word responses. If a salesperson asks ten close-ended questions about bedrooms, price range, etc, he or she is only going to receive ten isolated pieces of information. However, the salesperson that asks questions that are strategic and open-ended might find that the answers yield a much deeper understanding of the customer.

For example, a sales counselor might ask, "How many bedrooms are you looking for?" This is important information to ascertain, but the question is closed and brings about a one-word answer: "Four." However, if the question is posed as, "Tell me what's most important to you in a new home. I want to be able to point you in the right direction," the answer will be something like this: "We're looking for a one-story because I have a bum knee. We need at least three bedrooms but preferably four, so I can have a home office. We'd love to have a big kitchen that opens to a family room. And a three-car garage would be wonderful if we can get it."

Note that the open-ended question elicited seven significant pieces of information. That's the beauty of it. We learn so much more when we do not limit the prospect to a one-word response.

What does all this have to do with selling in a tough market? Plenty. As sales counselors, we need every advantage we can get in order to stand out and not be eliminated from contention. When we know our customers at a deeper level than our competitors do, we will discover why our homes and our location meet their very specific needs while the competitor does not. Then, if we get caught in an incentive battle with a different community, we have the upper hand. If customers take the competitor's incentive, they also have to take the competitor's inferior offering!

Dr. John Musser, Psychologist, www.salespotential.com

"Mediocre performers use sales presentations that do not engage the buyer in a way that the salesperson can identify the challenges that person is facing. They are not curious enough. They do not probe enough. Then, they do not engage powerfully enough to assist the buyer to overcome their challenge and take action to achieve their goal. They are too willing to back off. They take customers at their word without challenging their thinking."

POSING THE QUESTIONS

Not only are there wrong questions to ask, but there are wrong ways to ask questions. When I watch mystery shop tapes, one of the most egregious mistakes salespeople make during the opening conversation is committing to their next question while the prospect is still answering the last question. The salesperson asks a question; the prospect responds; and the salesperson immediately asks a different and unrelated question. Here's an example right from a mystery shop tape:

Sales Counselor:	*"Why are you looking at this particular location?"*
Buyer:	*"We really need to be near an airport."*
Sales Counselor:	*"Okay. Do you have children?"*

Stop the tape! Where did that come from? How did we transition from being near an airport (an interesting clue to the life and lifestyle of the prospect) to whether there are children? Why would a salesperson ask this question?

In this case, the salesperson responded in this way because while the customer was answering her first question, the salesperson was thinking of what she was going to ask next. This is a very common issue in the sales office. Salespeople often get so stuck on their next question that they miss very important messages that customers are trying to send. The non-sequitur is a signal that the sales counselor really was never listening in the first place.

> *"Most people do not listen with the intent to understand.*
> *They listen with the intent to respond."*
> **Stephen Covey**

What the salesperson doesn't realize is that oftentimes the customer is thinking, "She's not listening, and if she's not listening she cannot understand who I am and what I need." Not listening – and by "listening," I mean actively and attentively listening – is a major problem in many sales office conversations. Salespeople who are not listening miss out on incredibly important information, and they miss out on the opportunity to truly understand their customers.

When opening questions are thought-out and applied using sound strategy, something amazing happens. The set pattern of questions allows the salesperson to fully engage with the customers and to fully comprehend their answers. If you have thought through your questioning strategy, you are able to concentrate completely on the conversation because you are not otherwise mentally occupied by formulating your next question! You are liberated from this mental burden.

Now is the time to consider your own questioning pattern. Do you have one, and is it strategic? Have you ever sat down and planned the questions that you intend to ask during a sales conversation? What are the most important questions? What should your strategy look like? Figure out what works for you, and make use of this important tactic.

RELATIONSHIP-BUILDING QUESTIONS

When it comes to questioning strategies, most people's first impulse is to ask discovery questions. In a tough market, it is crucial that the salesperson understands the customer, but it is far more critical that the salesperson begins to build a trust relationship with the customer. Therefore, sales conversations should not start with sales questions; they should begin with trust questions.

Poor opening questions were addressed in the last chapter. Here, we're talking about good opening questions. Good opening questions vary as much as the great salespeople who ask them. To figure out what your opening question should be, ask yourself what your goal is and what you're trying to accomplish. If you're trying to establish a relationship, don't ask a housing-needs question.

Here are some opening questions that might work for you:

- "So, you're out shopping for a home. How's it going?"

- "You look tired. Can I get you a cold bottled water?"

- "Welcome to our community. How is your day going?"

- "Thanks for taking the time to visit us. Are you well today?"

- "Home shopping can be fun, or it can be stressful. How are you holding up?"

- "You could have stopped anywhere, but you stopped here. Thanks for coming in."

- "Do you enjoy your [type of car they are driving]?"

- "Are those your children? How old are they?"

- "I love your sweater." (Okay, I'm not a big "I love your sweater" guy myself, but I've seen it strike up wonderful conversations!)

The most important thing is that you pick a question that is comfortable for you and that sticks to the trust-building strategy.

Christine Woodcock, Owner, WRE Services, Seattle, Washington

"Have we forgotten the fundamental reason why people buy homes? In the normal markets people bought homes because they loved them and wanted to improve their lifestyle in some way by owning that home. Years of investors (whether professional investors or homeowners who shopped for their home the way they shopped for the best stock purchase) and hot market conditions got many of us off track on our sales approach. We sold appreciation and investment potential, instead of selling dinner parties in this new kitchen and Johnny playing at the neighborhood park. We forgot that in order to be effective in selling lifestyle benefits, we had to get to KNOW our customers and UNDERSTAND their goals and desires. Only by investing in a relationship with them can we hope to help them to find the right home, fall in love with the home and want to own it."

STRUCTURING YOUR QUESTIONS

When you move from trust-building questions to discovery questions, you need to have a strategy in mind to determine both the questions you will ask and the order in which you will ask them. Discovery questions give salespeople the edge in a tough market because they give them the advantage of deep understanding.

Here are the steps to creating a set of discovery questions that works for you:

Step One: Below are eight categories of questions for you to ask. They are listed alphabetically. Consider how you would ask them sequentially in a sales conversation, and number the categories from one (1) to eight (8), according to what you want to learn first.

- Ability (Can they afford to buy? Have they talked to a lender?)

- Dissatisfaction (What is wrong with their current situation?)

- Experience (How long have they been looking? What do they know?)

- Motivation (Why are they thinking about buying a new home?)

- Needs (What are the "must-have" items on their list?)

- Status (Do they have a home to sell? Can they buy today?)

- Urgency (When do they want to move?)

- Wants (What are the "would-really-like-to-have" items on their list?)

Step Two: After you have numbered the categories, make a list using the first letter of each category. So, for example, your list might be D-A-M-T-N-S-W-U. You can write that list of letters on a piece of paper and keep it on your desk as a constant study aid and memory refresher. You need only remember the categories of the questions, not the actual questions. Knowing the first letter will help to keep the list fresh in your mind.

Step Three: Below is a list of questions for each category. Find a question for each category that works for you, or create one of your own. If you're creating your own questions, form your questions to be open-ended whenever possible. Open-ended questions yield the most complete answers.

Ability Questions
- "What do you do for a living?"

- "Will you be financing the home or paying cash?"

- "Have you investigated your financing options?"

- "Where will your down payment come from?"

Dissatisfaction Questions
- "What triggered your search for a new home?"
- "What is it about your current home that isn't working for you?"
- "What in your current situation needs changing?"
- "What specifically do you want to change about your current living situation?"

Experience Questions
- "How long have you been looking for a home?"
- "Is this your first home, or have you owned previously?"
- "How much do you understand about the process of buying a new home?"
- "Have you seen anything you like in your home search?"

Motivation Questions
- "Why are you moving?"
- "What was it that first got you thinking about buying a new home?"
- "What is it about your current home that isn't working for you?"
- "What is it that has you out looking for a new home?"

Needs Questions (keep them open-ended!)
- "What is most important for you in a new home?"
- "Are there any 'must-haves' on your list?"
- "Do you have any specific needs in mind?"
- "What is most important to you in the home itself?"

Status Questions
- "Is there anyone else involved in this decision?"

- "Do you have a home that you need to sell?"

- "What issues need to be resolved before you can purchase a home?"

Urgency Questions
- "When were you hoping to move into your new home?"

- "Do you have a set timeframe for moving, or are you flexible?"

- "Will your move date be determined by school schedules or some other issue?"

Wants Questions
- "Describe the home that you are hoping to find."

- "What is it about a home that will make you say, 'Yes, this is it!'?"

- "Tell me a little about your dream home."

- "Is there something you've seen in other homes that you wish you had in yours?"

<u>*Step Four*</u>: You have now structured your ideal opening questions, but you don't need to memorize anything but the categories. Just memorize the order of the letters and the categories that they stand for. It might help to write the letters in order on a piece of paper and tape it to your desk.

Once you have the categories memorized, you can ask a question that applies to that category and then sit back and listen to the customer's answer. You don't have to be thinking about the next question you'll ask because the next question is already set. Your mental energy is freed up to listen and, most importantly, to understand.

THE SIDE BENEFIT FOR YOU: FLEXIBILITY

The last thing in the world that I would want to suggest is that the sales presentation should be rigid and scripted. Not so. The overly scripted and perfectly canned presentation is fatally flawed because it does not take into account the needs of the customer. If I sell the way that I want to sell, regardless of the way that the customer wants to buy, whom am I serving?

On the other hand, the unplanned, free-flowing questions that are not strategically designed do nothing to enhance the experience. The salesperson that makes up the entire presentation on the fly is in no position to serve the best interests of the customer (or the company, for that matter).

However, having a set pattern of questioning frees up the sales conversation to be more organic. Because you will not be confined to thinking up the next question, you can deviate from the plan when it is appropriate. If a mini-tangent will lead to a deeper understanding of the customer's needs, you can follow it, knowing that you will get back on track momentarily. All you have to do is take a quick glance at the mental checklist and say to yourself, "Okay, I last asked a motivation question, so now it's time to ask a needs/wants question."

In time, this will become second nature; you won't even have to think about it. It's like a football team practicing their game plan or a lawyer laying out his line of questioning for a witness. A thought-out strategy is prepared in advance, and it is well rehearsed. It makes sense.

The understanding that you will gain will give you the decided edge in a tough market. You will simply understand your customers better than your competitors will, and the customers will know it!

Breaking Through to the Under-Communicator

When you have a prospect that just won't open up and answer the questions, try this: "May I take thirty seconds and give you a general overview of the community?" This question tells the buyer that he is in control, and it makes a valuable offer to him. Virtually any prospect who is looking for a home will say, "Yes."

In that thirty-second discussion, make sure you are checking in with your prospect to understand his needs. For example, "We have everything from three to five bedroom homes. How many were you looking for?" Or, "Our homes start in the $340's and go up to $450's. Is that the price you had in mind?"

You'll find this effective in getting the quiet types into a comfortable place.

SUMMARY

All of the suggestions given above can be boiled down to your sales philosophy. Is it product-centered, or is it customer-centered? If your sales philosophy is product-centered, then you'll do most of the talking. If your sales philosophy is customer-centered, the customer will talk, and you will listen and understand.

When you structure your opening questions, you free up mental space, and this new mental bandwidth is dedicated in full to truly understanding your prospect.

> *"Until you are influenced by my uniqueness,*
> *I will not be influenced by your opinion."*
> **Stephen Covey**

THOUGHT-PROVOKERS

1. *Do I make up questions on the fly more than I should? Could I benefit from planning out my opening line of questions?*

2. *Do I struggle with listening and retaining what I have heard from a prospect? Might a structured line of questioning free me up to listen more intently?*

3. *Are there specific things that I need to learn about my customers that I am not learning now? What questions would help me to gain a better understanding of my prospects?*

Chapter Five:
Taking Control of the Encounter

Husband:	*"Now, we're going into a sales office and there's gonna be a salesperson there. Remember – no emotions. I want to show 'em that I'm in control. I've had it up to here with these pushy salespeople telling me what to like, what to do, what to think. I'm gonna show 'em who's boss!"*
Wife:	*"Whatever you say, dear."*
Salesperson:	*"Welcome to Willowbrook, and thanks for visiting. I know you had a lot of choices of where you wanted to visit and you came here – we really appreciate that. And I promise to make this as enjoyable an experience as I can. You are the boss, and I am here to take care of you."*
Husband:	*"Hold me."*

In a strong market, salespeople feel comfortable taking control, and they do so with ease and confidence. After all, the customer needs the salesperson, and everyone knows it. In a tough market, an overbearing salesperson is the customer's worst fear. However, many salespeople interpret this apprehension as their cue *not* to take control. This is the wrong approach! While customers won't come right out and say it, they need the help of a capable salesperson.

Would you not agree with me that when you walk onto a used car lot, you are automatically uncomfortable because the person you need the most is the person you like the least? Now transfer that concept into the new home sales office. The customers don't know you from a stranger on the street, but they need you just the same. They are not thinking to themselves, "Gee, I sure hope this salesperson controls the conversation," but deep down they need you to do just that.

Too many salespeople, especially yielding salespeople, approach the conversation with this thought: "I have all the answers, so if you have all the right questions, I will be happy to help." Their rationale is that peppering the customer with questions can be pushy, intrusive, and abrasive, so they hang back and wait for the customer to take the lead. This approach puts far too much pressure on the customer to think up those good questions, a task for which they are often under-qualified.

Here is a typical opening conversation in a sales office in a challenging market:

Sales Counselor:	*"How can I help you today, sir?"*
Customer:	*"Just looking around. What are your incentives?"*

Why does the customer ask an incentive question right out of the gate? He does this because the salesperson forces him to do so! The customer is forced to come up with some kind of response to the salesperson, and so he simply parrots what he has heard in other sales offices. He doesn't know what else to ask!

It is critical that we as salespeople control the early sales office conversation. Too many salespeople equate control with manipulation, and this is simply not the case. When we take control, we guide the prospect on the journey that is in his or her best interest. We are sales leaders, and we are helping people to get to places that they cannot get to on their own. That's why we are there!

It is simply too difficult for customers to take control on their own. When the salesperson allows the customer to control the conversation, the result is an awkward pause, during which the customer is attempting to come up with an intelligent question. See for yourself. Tape record your own conversations with customers and listen for the awkward pauses. It will sound something like this:

Customer:	*"So, how are the schools?"*
Sales Counselor:	*"Excellent. We have really good schools here."*
(Awkward pause)	
Customer:	*"Um, okay. Is the area safe?"*
Sales Counselor:	*"Indeed. It is very safe."*
(Awkward pause)	
Customer:	*"Okay....."*

You see where we are? When we force the customer to control the conversation, we do so by forcing them to think up all the right questions. Talk about high-pressure sales! How long do you think that sale will move forward before the customer looks for an opportunity to move on?

We take the lead because it is in our customer's best interest. Think of the doctor who asks you a myriad of questions before offering a diagnosis. The questions are designed to give the doctor a complete understanding of your situation so as to provide the right diagnosis and then the correct remedy. This concept applies to the top performing sales counselor quite nicely.

"The key to successful leadership today is influence, not authority."
Kenneth Blanchard

"A leader is a dealer in hope."
Napoleon Bonaparte

BARRIERS TO TAKING THE LEAD IN THE SALES PROCESS

When sales counselors struggle in taking the lead in the sales process, their woes generally can be pinpointed as originating in at least one of these areas:

1.   A poorly planned questioning strategy

We discussed this in Chapter Four, but it is important in the context of this chapter as well. If you don't have a strategic questioning plan, you will be forced to "wing it" in the questioning process. Eventually, winging it will become a dead-end street. Again, there's too much pressure on the customer to help you with the sales process. Great salespeople have a plan, which works like a roadmap. Using a roadmap helps both you and your "passengers" feel comfortable with your ability to navigate. In the event of an unexpected roadblock, the roadmap tells you how to get around it and continue to stay on course.

Let me make this pitch one more time. If you've never thought through your opening sequence – if you cannot recite your sales strategy – go back to Chapter Four and follow the instructions found there. You simply cannot be an effective sales leader without a planned questioning strategy.

2.   Failure to ask the deeper discovery questions

In Chapter Four we talked about some of the most important questions to ask early in the process, but we don't have to stop there. Many salespeople ask the basic questions and then launch right into demonstration mode. Real customer knowledge comes from asking deeper and more profound questions.

You see, the top performer can ascertain bedroom count, price point, and location just like everyone else, but the real reason they will buy his or her home goes much deeper than just these considerations. There are profound and emotional considerations that go into choosing one three-bedroom, two-bath, one-story home over another, and only the wise salesperson will seek to discover these issues.

Jim Suth, Sales Trainer, Danville, California

"Listen! When you had 50 traffic and were selling 2 or 3 a week, I left you alone. No sales in the last 3 weeks and you had only 8 traffic? You had better know everything about those traffic units short of their birth weight!"

It is always in your best interest to ask deeper and more intriguing questions throughout the process. It's good for your understanding of the customer, but it also serves to keep your conversations fresh. That's particularly important in a tough market where the negative influences can take their mental toll.

Here are some sample questions that could provide great benefits in the way of understanding, but are rarely asked in the new home sales presentation:

- "When your best friend comes over, where do you spend time?"
- "Are you more of an indoor person or an outdoor person?"
- "Is there a favorite piece of furniture in your home? What makes this piece of furniture special?"
- "What is more important to you: the floorplan or the location?"
- "Tell me about your pets; how do they live in your home?"
- "When you entertain, is it more formal or informal? And what does that look like?"
- "If there was one thing about your current home you could replicate in your new home, what would it be?"

- "When you go to your best friend's home, is there something that makes you say, 'I really wish I had that in my home'?"

Consider for a moment what some of the answers to these questions might be and also where those answers might lead the conversation. Can you see how this might open up all kinds of interesting and exciting opportunities to know your customer on a much deeper level?

You might consider brainstorming a list of questions that are unique and special and that do not often get asked in the new home sales office. Ask for help from your peers at a sales meeting; you'll find this to be an interesting and provocative topic.

3. Talking too much

This is a huge problem in new home sales because nursing and feeding our egos through talking too much can turn into complete conversation dominance. The fact is that we as salespeople need to have a certain amount of self-confidence in order to be effective at our jobs. But when that self-confidence crosses the line and becomes the need to be heard, we will quickly find that the people around us check out of the conversation.

However, not all salespeople who have problems with talking too much do so because of an over-inflated ego. For many sales counselors this habit is actually a defense mechanism. Often a salesperson is uncomfortable asking a prospect questions for fear that he or she will come off as nosy or invasive and will turn instead to a strategy of telling. This is the reason for most of the feature-dumping that takes place in sales offices and model homes.

In the sales office conversation, you should be focusing on talking just twenty-five percent of the time. During this stage of the sale, you should be much more concerned with understanding customers than with loading them down with facts and figures. In the model demonstration, the conversation should be evenly balanced; you should be talking only fifty percent of the time. In other words, you should be listening at least as much as you are talking.

How do you talk only fifty percent of the time in the demonstration without creating the aforementioned awkward pauses? By asking the deeper questions. You don't control the sale by talking. You control it by asking and listening. Anytime you come to an awkward pause, immediately ask another question; this will always serve to keep the conversation natural.

"Don't talk unless you can improve on the silence."
New England Proverb

"One who never asks either knows everything or knows nothing."
Malcolm Forbes

THE TRAFFIC LIGHT RULE OF THUMB

Here's a handy way to evaluate your own talking tendencies. This comes from my career coach, Marty Nemko (www.martynemko. com):

"During the first thirty seconds of an utterance, your light is green: your listener is probably paying attention. During the second thirty seconds, your light is yellow: your listener may be starting to wish you'd finish. After the one-minute mark, your light is red. Yes, there are rare times you should 'run a red light': when your listener is obviously fully engaged in your missive. But usually, when an utterance exceeds one minute, with each passing second, you increase the risk of boring your listener and having them think of you as a chatterbox, windbag, or blowhard."

CONTROLLING THROUGH QUESTIONS

Control should be something that is shared. You control the questions, and your customers control the answers. This is the balance that is both comfortable and beneficial *for all parties.*

Think back to your structured questions from Chapter Three. Now, consider this opening dialogue in the sales presentation:

Sales Counselor:	*"Welcome! Thanks for coming by. I'm Jeff, and you are…?"*
Prospect:	*"Hi, I'm Robert."*
Sales Counselor:	*"A pleasure. So you're out shopping for a new home. Are you having fun?"*
Prospect:	*"I don't know about fun. There's a lot to see. But it's going all right."*
Sales Counselor:	*"Got it. So why are you moving?"*
Prospect:	*"We need more space, and we've been looking at this area. We just couldn't afford it until the prices came down."*
Sales Counselor:	*"Good for you! And you're right – it is a great buying opportunity right now. Tell you what – I want to be able to point you in the right direction. Tell me what's most important to you in a new home."*
Prospect:	*"Well, it's my wife and me and our two kids. We'd like four bedrooms because we get houseguests from time to time. We'd prefer a two-story, and we'd love it if the master bedroom wasn't right next to the other bedrooms."*
Sales Counselor:	*"Got it. Anything else on your must-have list?"*
Prospect:	*"If we could get something near a park, that would be great. We have big dogs that like to run."*
Sales Counselor:	*"Cool. What kind of dogs do you have?"*
Prospect:	*"We have two chocolate labs that have a lot of energy."*

Sales Counselor:	*"Outstanding. I have a home and location in mind that seems like what you've described. Do you have a time frame in mind for when you wanted to move in?"*
Prospect:	*"Doesn't matter. We're renting now, so when we find the home and the price, we're good."*

Let's stop there for a moment. This is more or less the presentation that I use when I work the floor of a sales office. Of course, this isn't the *only* way to makes a sales presentation. It's just the opening strategy that I've honed over the years. But I want you to notice something here. Note that I am really just four categories into my opening questioning strategy (motivation, needs, wants, and timing). But in those few questions, how many points of information have I gained from my prospect? I count sixteen valuable pieces of information – in a process that has taken less than sixty seconds!

But here is the critical question: who is in control? We both are! I control the questions; he controls the answers. I am in the lead, and we are following my sales agenda, but we are doing it in *his best interests*.

One other point about that conversation: Where in that dialogue did the incentive question come up? It didn't! The incentive question didn't come up because I structured the questions to avoid that topic. As the salesperson, I didn't allow that question to be asked. (And what do we do when the customer does bring up the incentive conversation? We read Chapter Eleven!)

Is that conversation unnatural? No, actually it works quite well for both parties. Customers are relieved that the pressure is off of them. They can simply respond by talking about their favorite subject – themselves.

KEY CONTROL TOSS-UP MOMENTS

Where do salespeople tend to give up control in the sales conversation? Below are some critical moments when control is a toss-up. Use this as a self-evaluative checklist, and truly consider whether you might have some improvement opportunities at hand. Control is at stake in these situations:

- When the salesperson asks, "Can I help you," or, "May I help you," or, "How may I help you?" (Chapter 3)

- When the conversation begins with a request for a registration card. (Chapter 4)

- When the customer is peppered with closed-ended questions. (Chapter 4)

- When the salesperson launches into a long-winded discourse on the homes. (Chapter 5)

- When customers are sent to models unaccompanied. (Chapter 7)

- When the salesperson fails to ask engaging soft-close questions throughout the tour. (Chapter 7)

- When the salesperson fails to use the Plan Close question. (Chapter 7)

- When the salesperson asks, upon returning from the model tour, "Did you have any questions?" (Chapter 5)

- When customers are sent to the site unaccompanied. (Chapter 8)

- When customers are not asked closing questions during the site tour. (Chapter 8)

- When the salesperson bails out of the final close. (Chapter 11)

STAYING IN CONTROL THROUGHOUT THE ENCOUNTER

It's one thing to start in control, but staying in control presents its own challenges. To stay in control, you should end every statement with a question whenever possible. When you overcome an objection, ask a question. When you demonstrate a value point, ask a question. When you answer a question from your customer, ask another question.

I'm not talking about manipulation here, which is often taught in old school sales training. Here's an example of sales manipulation:

Customer:	*"How much will the expanded family room cost?"*
Sales Counselor:	*"What is it worth to you?"*
Customer:	*"Huh? I just want to know the cost of that option."*
Sales Counselor:	*"Is the expanded family room important to you?"*
Customer:	*"Why would I be asking otherwise? What's its cost?"*
Sales Counselor:	*"What is more important to you – cost or value?"*
Customer:	*"What is less painful to you – a fat lip or a black eye?"*

Answering a question with another question is an old technique, and it is usually based on the manipulation of the customer. I reject that strategy in all but a few cases. An effective, question-based selling process is not about manipulation. It's about leadership. Salespeople lead when customers follow in directions that make sense for them. In the question-based leadership selling process, when customers answer questions in a way that indicates that the salesperson is leading them in the wrong direction, the salesperson knows that it's time for an immediate course correction. If you, as the salesperson, ask questions, you will know this as you go.

Here's one last tip for working on leading the sale: tape record your presentation. One of the best investments you can make for your career is the purchase of a small digital recorder. Record the opening few minutes of a sales office conversation and listen back to determine whether you are in control of the sales process. Listen for the non-sequiturs, for the missed opportunities, for awkward pauses, and for the times when you are just droning on without engaging the customer. This is an invaluable method of self-instruction on your own performance. (Check with your sales manager about company and/or regional policy regarding this practice.)

Bill Pisetsky, VP Sales and Marketing, Los Angeles, California

"Buying a home is an incredibly emotional endeavor. Understanding and controlling the mindset of the customer is all important. How do we do that? It starts with us! No matter what the market, 'sell from strength'. Feel good about what you are selling. If you do, it is an easier sell. If you do not, good luck............it will be the toughest sale you'll ever make. As a sales person, you have incredible power. Your customer watches your every move and listens to your every word. Know your stuff!"

SUMMARY

Taking control is something we do in our customer's best interest. It's about leadership, about taking people to places that they cannot get to on their own. It is a valuable gift that we provide for our customers. Don't look at it as manipulation, but rather as a valuable service.

THOUGHT-PROVOKERS

1. *How deep are your discovery questions? Are there questions you could be asking that give you a much broader sense of the character, needs, and desires of your customers?*

2. *Do you believe that you have a problem with talking too much during the sales presentation? What one technique could you implement today that would attack this concern?*

3. *Are there key control toss-up moments that you feel you might be able to work on? What specifically can you do today to overcome those issues?*

Chapter Six:
Protecting and Defending Value

Customer:	*"I want a big discount."*
Salesperson:	*"Of course, who doesn't? But I'm assuming you want it on a home you love, right?"*
Customer:	*"I can just tell you that PoorBuilt Homes down the street is offering a $200,000 incentive if I buy today. Can you match that?"*
Salesperson:	*"So you're saying that if I don't match their incentive that you will go buy the one home in the entire area that no one else wants, correct?"*
Customer:	*"I'm saying I want a screaming deal."*
Salesperson:	*"On a bad house."*
Customer:	*"Hey, don't try that logic stuff on me. I'm perfectly happy being irrational."*

*"There is hardly anything in the world that some man can't make
a little worse and sell a little cheaper, and the people
who consider price only are this man's lawful prey."*
John Ruskin

A customer enters into a new home sales office and the first thing she sees is a white board, just inside the front door – you can't miss it.

Across the top of the board are the words, "Home of the Week" (although it just as appropriately could read, "Home of the *Weak*"). She notes the "was-is" pricing strategy, with the "was" price crossed out (using a red pen, of course). In this case, the sign reads, "~~Was $399,990,~~" and, "Now $319,990." Next she sees bullet points that list exactly how desperate the builder is, indicated by a willingness to toss everything – yes, even the upgraded kitchen sink – on the deal. Now let's add a cloud off to the side of the white board that contains the following phrase: "Ask about Special Financing." Sound familiar?

Wait, it gets worse. The salesperson looks at her and says, "I have just spoken with my sales manager, and he sounds desperate. Do you want my advice? Why don't you make me an offer?" Think I'm making this scenario up? Think again. This really happens – we've seen this exact scenario on a mystery shop tape.

If you were this customer, what would you be prepared to offer for this home? $290,000? $250,000? $230,000 and a pool? A customer, sensing blood in the water, might make an offer but ask for a fifty percent price reduction. Insulted, the salesperson would respond by saying something like, "How dare you assault the value of my home in such a way!" (Sorry, pal – you started it!)

Everyone can agree that in a tough market value is under attack. However, is it possible that the attack starts with the *seller*, not the buyer? As counterintuitive as this might seem, frequently it is the case. In a tough market if you are not fiercely protective of your own value proposition, you cannot win the value battle. And if you lose the value battle, you'd better have the highest incentives around – that is the only way to land a new sale.

UNDERSTANDING VALUE

In the world of sales, we need to come to grips with this criti-cal principle: Value becomes valuable when the customer decides it's valuable. In other words, the value discussion means nothing until we know the customer's sense of value. The problem is that salespeople sell their own versions of value, often when they've not yet ascertained what is valuable to the customer. Remember this principle:

"Value" is a buyer word, not a seller word.

How do we know the customer's sense of value? Through strate-gic discovery. This chapter goes hand-in-hand with our discussions in Chapter Four. If you've not thought through your strategic discovery process, the rest of this chapter will mean little to you.

Let me offer an example: I own a painting, and it is very valu-able. It's an oil painting of a hillside landscape, with a quaint church on a country road and mountains in the background. When I see this painting, I want to be in that setting. If I asked you to make me an offer to purchase this painting, how much would you offer? As you're reading, right this moment, come up with a number.

Let me add some additional information about the painting. It is an original and signed by the artist. It has never been duplicated; there are no prints in circulation. As the seller, my guess is that it would sell for around $5,000 in a gallery. Now how much would you pay? Again, come up with a number in your mind. Did your opinion change? Did your value perception change?

The truth is that you could offer me $50,000 for this painting, and I would not sell it. It's not for sale. The artist is Kevin Shore, my son, and he painted the country landscape as a present for my wife and me. It's phenomenal, and there is no price at which I would part with it.

THREE ASPECTS OF VALUE

In the above example, we can see that three different contributing factors make up value: inherent value, scarcity, and personal connection.

In the sale of a home, the inherent value speaks to what the buyer sees or perceives, aspects of the property including features and amenities. Inherent value is partially objective and partially subjective. Objectively, the features of a property are valuable. However, subjective judgments like quality perceptions, aesthetic attraction, and personal taste all factor into inherent value.

Scarcity speaks to how rare an item is. Is it mass-produced or custom-built? In new home sales, hot markets are known for and driven by scarcity. In fact, in hot markets the scarcity factor trumps inherent value. People will make compromises and buy homes that they don't love just so they don't miss out. An important part of the new home salesperson's job is to build scarcity. This is done most effectively by only selecting a single site (see Chapter Nine).

Finally, personal connection drives personal value. Everyone owns something that is valuable to them only on the basis of personal connection – a ticket stub, a photograph, a diary or journal, an antique. Personal connection value is difficult to measure, but it is an incredibly powerful motivator. For example, I won't buy a home with eight-foot ceilings simply because I would have no place for an antique armoire that my wife and I own. In this case, ceiling height is a deal-breaker, not based on the feature (ceiling height), but on personal connection (space for my armoire).

When salespeople know a great deal about their customers, they can find opportunities for understanding their clients' personal connections. This will lead to helping picture the perfect backyard scene for young children, finding a place for an heirloom baby grand, or visualizing a craft room.

When you are trying to sell a home to a given prospect you must be aware of these three value components. To get a picture of how this works in real-time, think of prospects with whom you are currently working. Try to determine what feature values are important to them; try to think of what accounts for scarcity in what they are seeing; and, most importantly, try to determine their sense of personal connection. If you can do this with every strong prospect, you are well on your way to landing the sale. Moreover, when you consider these three points with every potential homebuyer, you can tailor your sales presentation to address each of these three areas.

COMMUNITY VALUE: THE UNIQUE SELLING PROPOSITION

One way to maximize the value of a property is to promote the Unique Selling Proposition (USP) in the community. Every community has a specific USP, but not every salesperson knows what it is. I go into sales offices all the time and ask about it. Most salespeople respond by saying, "Great value!" or, "Excellent quality." These answers are wrong because they are generic. There is nothing unique about great value or excellent quality. If a salesperson cannot point to something very special and very specific about a community, then it will never be unique, and thus, it will carry little specific value.

In a challenging market these "it" factors define and separate. They give the customer a reason to love one community and discount another. If nothing stands out in a community, the customer will quickly eliminate that community as a housing option.

The USP answers the question, "Why do we rock? What is it about our community that a customer cannot get if they buy anywhere else?" Here is the critical question that will help you determine what is specifically distinctive about your home: *If your home and your strongest competitor's home were both free, why would a customer choose yours?* The answer to this question will be the USP, and you should know it off the top of your head.

The USP will always include superlatives like *largest*, *lowest*, or *only*. Check out the following examples:

- "We have the *largest* homesites in a five-mile radius."

- "We have the *lowest* priced single-family homes in this master-planned community."

- "We have the *only* pool-sized lots in this area."

- "We are the *closest* new home community to the light rail station."

- "We are the *only* community where you can walk to the school, the park, and Starbucks."

When developing your USP, you might try talking to your land acquisition directors. When they bought the land, you can be sure that there was a clearly defined USP in mind.

Most importantly, as a salesperson you must ask yourself, "Am I thoroughly convinced of the value of my own product?" If the answer is anything other than a resounding "Yes!", you've got some research to do.

PROTECTING VALUE: HANDLING THE INCENTIVE QUESTION

In a tough market, the greatest attack on value comes in the form of the incentive discussion. Salespeople need to be adept at handling this conversation quickly and confidently. Many salespeople wrongly begin discussing incentives right out of the gate. They see it as adding value, and they use it as an attention-getter. They think, "If I share my value immediately, I'll stand out from the rest."

Rich Ambrosini, Homebuilding Division President, Concord, California

"It absolutely drives me crazy when a salesperson wants to talk about incentives right away, without any attempt to talk more important things first. "Why are you here today?" "What are you looking for?" "What's most important to you?" Too often the sales counselor lets the homebuyer dictate the conversation."

The truth is that when people buy according to incentives, the home is clearly undervalued. Why do we – why does anyone – give away $20,000 in incentives? We do it because we don't think we can sell the home if we only give away $19,000! We try to compensate for unfavorable scale comparisons by adding financial incentives.

Oftentimes this weakens, not sweetens, the deal because . . .

- If a salesperson needs to add incentives, the deal probably wasn't that strong in the first place.

- The deal may get better in the future.

- More variables will confuse the overall value perception.

At the time of this writing, it is not unusual in many higher-priced markets to see incentives of $200,000 or more on a stated price of $800,000. One would think that these homes would be gobbled up like hotcakes. Not so. Oftentimes, the huge incentives only confuse the value equation in the prospect's mind. In fact, there is no specific connection yet proven between high incentives and high absorption rates!

Think about this from a customer's perspective. When a customer sees a $100,000 incentive, he or she knows instinctively that the builder is not doing this because he's one heckuva nice guy. The customer also knows that the builder didn't wake up one day and say, "This home isn't selling – let's put a $100,000 incentive on it." That home once had a $10,000 incentive, then $20,000, then $40,000, and so on. The customers can figure this out – they are being offered the highest incentive on *the home that no one else wants*! It is imperative, should you be in a position where a competitor has higher incentives than you are willing to give, that you remind prospects of this fact.

Until our customers need our homes for some other reason than the incentive, there is no reason to believe they will find enough urgency to purchase (see Chapter Seven).

COMMON MISSTEPS IN THE INCENTIVE DISCUSSION

1.   Sharing the incentive without being asked

Customer: *"I want to get some information."*

Salesperson: *"Great. Our prices start in the high 500's, and we have a $50,000 incentive."*

What's wrong with this approach to sharing the incentive? Everything! In the first place, the customer didn't even ask about incentives. This incentive-sharing approach isn't adding value; it's a price apology. In other words, in this discussion the customer hears, "Our homes start in the 500's, but there is no way they are worth that much. The market was going up and up and up. And my sales manager – he's crazy! He was calling me at home in the evening, telling me to raise prices. Well, things got a little out of hand, and the next thing you know, we're giving that money back."

I don't know how you're using your incentive, but here is the most fundamental concept for discussing incentives: Don't bring it up! The earlier you introduce it, the less value you get for it.

Incentives are expensive – don't give them away for cheap!

2. Sharing the incentive before value has been established

Customer:	*"What are your incentives?"*
Salesperson:	*"$50,000"*

This mini-discussion occurs all the time. Here the salesperson does nothing to defend the value proposition. She just answers the question. My friend and sales trainer Charlie Jenkins labels this tactic as "spilling your popcorn in the lobby."

If I wanted to make a deal with you and give you $50,000 off the price of the home that I live in right now, would you want to buy it? Of course not. You wouldn't buy it because you haven't seen it yet. I'm offering $50,000 on a concept. If this sounds like a bad idea to you, then you must also think that offering the incentive without having established value in the home you are selling is likewise a less-than-stellar strategy.

The principle is simple. The earlier in the process that the salesperson shares the incentives, the less value he will receive. If he blurts it out right away, he gets nothing. If he holds onto it, it becomes very valuable indeed. In other words,

Incentives make great closing tools, but they are lousy opening tools!

3. Failing to control the conversation

Top performers stand out by controlling the conversation, and they earn the opportunity to use the incentive discussion to their best advantage.

Many salespeople complain that customers ask the incentive question at the very beginning of the interaction. There are two reasons for this. First, customers are trained by other salespeople. Great salespeople follow a structured sales presentation because they have been trained, and they use what they learn. Buyers need a *buying* presentation, but they don't have the benefit of structured training. They learn their buyer/seller interaction strategies as they go, namely in other sales offices. They're not being mean, greedy, or manipulative. They're just parroting back what they heard in their last conversation with a salesperson. They don't know all the right questions to ask, so they ask what they think they're supposed to ask. They follow a script that has been written by another sales counselor.

Customers introduce the incentive question because salespeople sit back and wait for them to ask a question. Salespeople who don't control the conversation with their own questioning strategy are inviting the incentive discussion.

For example, a customer comes into your office.

You say, "Can I help you?"

She responds, "What are your incentives?"

What just happened? You abdicated control of the conversation. The customer didn't know what questions to ask, so she started with one that she's heard before.

What is the remedy? Control the conversation in order to defer the incentive question. Don't give the customer the opportunity to ask! If you're unclear on this, go back and read Chapter Four for a thorough discussion on controlling the conversation.

> ### Tracy Miller, Sales Trainer, Jacksonville, Florida
>
> *"An incentive is something that entices someone to make a decision. If you throw out the incentive before the customer has enough information to make a purchase decision, the incentive is now merely a price discount. Make sure the value discussion revolves around a home that matches the customers needs and wants. Find that home, and then close them with an incentive that fits their needs."*

THE LOGICAL USE OF INCENTIVES

Customers tend to be skeptical people. Everyone can be a bit skeptical when making major decisions; this is nothing more than a valid defense mechanism. It is logical for them to question all aspects of value.

It's not logical to offer an incentive without an explanation as to why you are offering the incentive in the first place. When an incentive is given without a reason, the customer invents a reason. He assumes that the incentive is a price apology – a discount. Don't give an incentive without giving a reason; it weakens the value proposition.

Always offer a reason as to why you are offering an incentive. Here are a few examples:

- "We have some homes that are going to be ready sooner than we expected, so we've added some value for those buyers who can move quickly."

- "Our customers tell us that they want to customize their own deals, so we set aside some incentives to let each customer put together the perfect terms for themselves."

- "Our customers tell us they'd prefer to hold onto their cash, so we offer incentives to pay for the closing costs."

- "Everyone wants to finish their own home differently. We offer incentives so that each customer can upgrade the home and finish it according to his or her personal taste."

"WHAT ARE YOUR INCENTIVES?" – ANSWERING THE QUESTION

When the question does come up in the sales office conversation, you'll need to be adept at deferring the discussion until the time comes when the incentive will add value (and this never happens in the initial conversation). Here are four approaches to consider:

1. Redefine your incentive as your USP.

   Answer: "Our incentives? We are the only gated community in the area at under $400,000." Or, "We have the largest homesites anywhere in this city."

   The key here is to deflect the conversation by talking about the *real* incentives, about the real reason people fall in love with your homes. Then you can say, "We have some financial incentives as well. We'll talk about that in a little while. So tell me, what is most important to you in your new home?" This last statement lets the customer know that you are planning on discussing incentives, but not at this time.

2. Make it depend on something else.

   Answer: "It can be thousands of dollars, but it varies according to floorplan and homesite location. Let's determine your preferences, and I'll go over the numbers with you."

3. Make them a deal.

   Answer: "We're less than five minutes from my telling you exactly what our incentives are. All you need to do is tell me if you like the home I show you. Deal?"

4. Ask a closing question.

   Answer: "Did you want to purchase a home? Because normally we talk about the terms of the sale when we sit down to write a contract. Is that what you wanted to do?"

SUMMARY

The customer's value perspective is the only perspective that really counts. We should "seek first to understand" the customer's sense of value, and only then can we sell effectively. Personal connection is the greatest value asset the customer has and the greatest opportunity for the top performing sales counselor to meet the prospect's deepest needs. If the sale gets bogged down in a discussion of what we are giving away (in other words, how big of a discount the customer can get), we will never protect the inherent value of home and community.

THOUGHT-PROVOKERS

1. *How often can you say that you truly understand your customer's deepest sense of personal value?*

2. *What do you tend to push the most in your own sales presentation: features, scarcity, or personal connection? Is this an area that you need to work on?*

3. *If your home and your closest competitor's home were both free, why would the customer move into yours?*

4. *Do you have a tendency to share the incentives too early in the process? Is there a tactic you could work on that would allow you to defer the conversation?*

Chapter Seven:
Getting to the Plan Selection

Salesperson:	*"Which floorplan did you like the best?"*
Customer:	*"The Jamison. No, wait…the Princenton. Hold on – definitely it was the Waterford. Or the Princenton. One of those three."*
Salesperson:	*"Do you struggle with making decisions?"*
Customer:	*"Never! No, wait…always. Hold on – sometimes…"*

> *"Plan your work, then work your plan."*
> **Anonymous**

From time to time I will ask a new home sales professional to share with me his or her sales strategy. "Tell me about your game plan, about how you move prospects along from the time they walk through the door to the time they write a contract." I'm not even going to suggest that there is one right answer to that question, but you would be surprised at how often I get the old "blank stare." It is clear in these cases that the salesperson has never really given any thought to a strategic sales presentation.

In a really strong market, a salesperson can get away with not having a strategic process. In this case, selling becomes far more reactive to the urgency that prospects bring with them into the process. By contrast, a challenged market presents a different set of demands – a salesperson must have a specific sales strategy in mind in order to maximize the opportunity. Those sales counselors without a road map to the sale can only hope to get lucky. Of course, luck is not much of a strategy. In fact, it's nothing more than a pipe dream, and it will only lead to disappointment when the market is not doing us any favors.

And so it would seem that the best presentations follow a strategy and that this strategy guides us from point to point throughout the sales process. If we can identify significant milestones as we go, we can be confident that we are making progress and that we are, in fact, headed in the right direction.

Let me share an analogy to give you a clearer picture: Suppose you are going on a three-hour drive that you've often made in the past. Let's suppose, for example, that you are driving on Interstate 5 from Los Angeles to San Diego. Along the way you'll pass some milestones – Disneyland, the 405 merge, San Juan Capistrano, and so on. Each milestone confirms that you are headed in the right direction and that you have proceeded further toward your destination.

But on the drive from L.A. to San Diego, there is one milestone that really stands out for me – Camp Pendleton, a Marine base on the Pacific coast. The significance of Camp Pendleton is that it represents the halfway mark of the drive. When I pass Pendleton, I am on the San Diego side of my journey, and I can anticipate that I will soon be at my destination.

CENTERING THE SALES PRESENTATION

What if we looked at the sale in the same way? What if we could identify similar milestones and even a significant halfway point? It seems to me that if we knew these landmarks, we could simply "drive" the sale from one step to the next, working toward the halfway point and launching from there to our destination.

For me, the sales presentation can be centered on one critically important question (think of this milestone as Camp Pendleton, if it helps). This one question represents the most significant landmark in the sales process, and when we pass this landmark (assuming the customer responded positively to the question), we are racing to the destination.

It's called the "Plan Close" question, and it is used like this: When I've walked someone through a model home or a blueprint, and I believe that we've found the right home for this prospect, I simply ask this question: "So, does this look like the right plan for you and your family?" That's it. No rocket science here. The question is simple, natural . . . and unbelievably powerful.

The Plan Close question is critical to the sales presentation because it establishes two facts. First, it clarifies for the salesperson what the customer has or has not accepted up to that point in the conversation. If the prospect answers with a "yes," he or she is telling the salesperson that value has been established in the home, the community, the price, and everything else discussed up to this point. Second, it tells the salesperson if the customer is ready to move to the next step. This is "go time"! It's a sprint from here to the finish line. It would be totally unnatural for the sale to stop at this point. The response from the customer demands a site tour and then a final close.

Before we go on, you might be thinking to yourself that this sounds like common sense, and I would agree with you. However, that which is common in sense is not always common in practice. The truth is that

I rarely hear that specific Plan Close question posed to a customer during a sales presentation. In my observations of sales presentations and shop tapes, it just doesn't come up all that often.

If this question is so important, why is it so often neglected by salespeople? This can only happen because the salesperson is operating on assumptions. She gets the buying signals from the customer. She doesn't feel that she needs to ask the Plan Close question because she believes that she already has the answer. An assumption is made. Even when the salesperson ends up being right in her assumptions, she could find herself in trouble.

This trouble originates in the fact that she has misunderstood one of the most fundamental principles regarding closing. Salespeople must not ask closing questions for their own benefit; they must ask closing questions for the benefit of the *homebuyer*! I don't ask for me; I ask for them! After all, which is more important, that I understand that this is the right plan choice for the buyer, or that the buyer hears himself acknowledge this important fact? When I assume the customer's plan selection and therefore neglect the closing question, I rob the customer of the opportunity to narrow down his search to just one particular floor plan.

This is a radical departure from the idea of closing as manipulation. Salespeople should not close with the purpose of directing the buyer into purchasing something that is not in the buyer's best interest. Salespeople should close because customers need to come to terms with their own value perceptions. When the Plan Close question goes unasked, customers are robbed of the self-affirmation that they receive when they realize that they have chosen the plan that works best for them.

THE PLAN CLOSE IN A CHALLENGING MARKET

In a tough market, salespeople cannot simply wait for a customer to display all the buying signals. Truthfully, buying signals are over-rated and better left forgotten. As we have said before, there is one legitimate buying signal – *the customer walked through your door*! You should assume that everyone who enters the sales office is there to purchase immediately. The beauty of the Plan Close question is that it gives you a target to work toward, and as long as the customer agrees with you along the way, you can continue to advance the sale.

The Plan Close question does more than it appears to do. When a customer says yes to the Plan Close, he is also agreeing to and accepting all of the information that was given in leading up to the Plan Close. In other words, the customer is not only agreeing that he likes Plan Two, but is also affirming his acceptance of almost everything that has been shared up to that point, including price, location, commute, payments, quality perception, warranty, status, and so on. Of course, this is great news. It means that the salesperson is more than halfway to the sale when the customer says yes to the Plan Close question. However, the news gets better from here. If the customer has accepted the plan, the price, the payments, the location, and so on, he is ready for the site tour. And the site tour is where the sale picks up steam. A "yes" to the Plan Close question means that it's time for the customer to select his one-of-a-kind homesite. In other words, it is time for him to buy a home.

Why is this so relevant in a challenging market? Because it places the emphasis on the home and its inherent value more than on the incentive or the "deal." It gives the prospect a reason to need your home more than she needs your competitor's, even if that competitor is offering a higher incentive. In a tough market, we are looking for any kind of personal urgency we can find. The urgency that comes with an emotional tie to one particular home is an incredibly strong motivator for the prospect.

My suggestion should be clear by now. You should be structuring your sales presentation around the Plan Close question. However, my second suggestion is that you should track your frequency of Plan Closes as a key factor in determining your sales progress. I believe that the Plan Close question can make a huge difference in your production levels, but you can find that out for yourself by tracking how often you ask this question. Track your frequency for four weeks. Then ask yourself, "How many times did I ask the Plan Close question, and what happened when I did?"

GETTING TO THE PLAN CLOSE

Would you agree with me that the easiest closing question to ask is the one to which you already know the answer? Isn't it far easier to ask someone if she likes the community, for example, if she's already made a number of positive comments about the area along the way?

This principle holds true for the Plan Close as well. We want this question to be simple and natural, and we want to ask it with confidence. That confidence comes when we have already ascertained that we have found the plan that best suits our customer's needs.

So let's spend some time trying to determine how we can lay out a strategy to get to that Plan Close in a simple and natural manner. To do this, I ask for your indulgence as we work backwards in the process. Let's begin with the goal in mind – getting a "yes" to the Plan Close question. How can we ask this question, boldly and confidently, with some certainty that the customer will respond positively? The best way to do this is to focus first on some important model demonstration closing questions called "Room Closes."

ROOM CLOSES

Closing should be a simple and natural part of the sales process. We want to focus on closing questions that should occur naturally along the path of the sale. In other words, we will look for closing attempts that normally and naturally pop up along the way. Keeping in mind the destination on which we are currently focused – the Plan Close – we need to determine what closing opportunities we can identify that lead us to that point.

The Room Close question is an incredibly powerful closing technique that causes your customers to close themselves! Remember that we do not ask closing questions primarily for our own benefit; we ask closing questions so that the customers can determine whether the value proposition works for them.

This is really quite simple. When I enter a given room in the home, I have a goal in mind – I will not leave the room without asking a closing question. It sounds something like this: "So does this kitchen look like it will work for you?" That's it. You can try to make it more sophisticated if you want to, but I wouldn't recommend it. The question does the trick. It forces the customers to come to grips with the value proposition – it works for them or it doesn't.

Do you see where I'm going with this? If I ask a Room Close question in every significant area of the home, and if the prospect answers affirmatively, where am I by the time the tour is complete? I am ready for the Plan Close! More importantly, I already know the answer to the Plan Close question. The customer will not say "yes" to every room in the home only to say "no" when it comes to the Plan Close!

Practice this. Make it your action plan. Determine right now that whenever you walk a prospect into a room of a home, you will not leave that room without asking a Room Close question.

THE ROOM-BY-ROOM DEMONSTRATION

Now let's focus on how we get to that Room Close question. Let me share with you a basic yet effective room-by-room demonstration method. The key to this method is that it is question-based. We want to talk minimally and to ask a maximum amount of questions.

Here are five simple steps for presenting a room-by-room demonstration:

1.   Ask for first impressions.

Resist your temptation to talk first. So many salespeople want to immediately offer their own first impressions of the room. This is a big mistake. The customer's value opinion is the one that counts! So ask him right away, "What are your first impressions?" If the customer loves it, he will say so, and in so doing he is closing himself! If he does not, he will let you know this as well. And really, do you want to drone on about how great a room is if the customer's initial impression is negative?

2.   Ask for specific likes

Avoid the temptation to feature-dump. Advanced sales technique says that top performing salespeople are strong in getting their *customers* to feature-dump! You want your customers to point out the things that they find valuable. In doing so, they continue to close themselves on the value in each room.

3.   Paint a lifestyle picture.

The purpose of the demonstration is not to point out features. It is to get the prospects at home in the product. Ask them about livability, about lifestyle scenes, and about future moments. Take what you have learned about your customers and offer it back to them in a life picture.

4. Point out a few key features (if necessary).

Yes, there might be a time to demonstrate features, but only if the customers are missing very important things that they wouldn't notice on their own. Keep it limited, however.

5. Close on the room.

Simply ask, "Does this room work for you?" That's it. You'll already know the answer if you've followed the first four steps. From here you can transition quite naturally to the next room of the home.

DEMONSTRATION TECHNIQUES FOR A TOUGH MARKET

Demonstrating is critical. Some salespeople get that, and some don't. For your own sake, get it! Some people are good at it, and some aren't. Get good!

Dan Koontz, VP Sales, Fresno, California

"When our sales associates conducted more home tours with our customers we sold more homes. When we improved our home tour sales skills and then conducted more home tours we sold even more homes. When we discovered the customers perception of value, improved our sales skills and conducted more model tours we sold the most homes of all."

Great salespeople connect with the core of what they do, which is building strong value perceptions and agreements. Unfortunately, many salespeople leave their customers to discover value on their own. This is a huge mistake. In a strong market, customers are convinced of value based on market urgency, but in a weak or balanced market, people must be shown and persuaded toward value. The bottom line is that a salesperson cannot be great in the long run if he or she does not demonstrate well.

Of course, demonstrating effectively brings benefits to you as the salesperson. It connects you with the core of who you are professionally, with your professional identity as a salesperson. Selling is what you do. When you neglect the core of who you are, your identity suffers. With it goes your confidence, and your abilities decline. Demonstrating models is the surest way to keep you on your toes.

Many salespeople do not demonstrate because they've never been shown how to do it well. But if you follow the room-by-room demonstration process, you should find that your technique improves dramatically.

Dan Koontz, VP Sales, Fresno, California

"The difference between simply walking a customer through a model home and conducting a professional model home tour is like the difference between a photo of Disneyland and actually going to Disneyland. The well-trained sales associate will make the home tour the exciting and emotionally driven event the customer is seeking. It is the most critical stage of the sales process."

COMMON MISTAKES IN THE MODEL DEMONSTRATION

1. Talking too much

Most salespeople think that they are *supposed* to talk a lot during the demonstration. This isn't a great strategy. As a salesperson, you should be doing the talking no more than fifty percent of the time. 50/50 is a good ratio because you don't want to talk the whole time, but you don't want silence either. The best strategy is to ask lots and lots of questions. In this way, you get your customer to identify value for you and for themselves.

2. Feature-dumping

Salespeople often feature-dump because they have no predetermined strategy, and so they talk about whatever they see. Feature-dumping is a mistake for three reasons. First, the customer is not going to retain everything you tell him or her. Second, as a salesperson, you become a walking brochure. Third, and most importantly, feature-dumping does not engage the prospective buyer. The bottom line is that you shouldn't rob your customers of their sense of discovery.

3. Standing in the wrong places

The wrong places for salespeople to stand during a model presentation include the following:

- In front of windows

- In the middle of the room

- In front of special features

- In a small room or hallway

The biggest issue we find here is that the salesperson is adding unwanted perspective for the prospect. When we stand in the wrong places, we draw attention away from the greatest value opportunities.

4. Neglecting closing opportunities

Too many salespeople see demonstrating as merely that – demonstrating or showing off value. Actually, demonstrating is the perfect opportunity to begin the closing process. In fact, if a salesperson is not closing throughout the demonstration, then the final close becomes impossible.

DEMONSTRATION TIPS AND TECHNIQUES

Here are some recommendations for building an effective demonstration method:

- Plan and practice your presentation. If you don't, you'll be forced to wing it. Winging it always leads to feature-dumping.

- Ask questions throughout the entire presentation. Let the questions lead you. Remember 50/50.

- Begin the demonstration outside the model. Take the opportunity to sell the architecture and the street scene. It's amazing how many salespeople overlook this opportunity. One-third of customers are more focused on location and exterior than any other feature. So, sell the street; sell how the home sits on the street; sell the status.

- Make the entrance into the home a "moment." Pause and lead the customer into taking it all in. This moment doesn't have to be syrupy, but it does need to be special.

- Let the prospect experience the initial impression of the home – get out of the way. Don't block the initial view of the entry. In addition, don't open the door for your customers; give them that tactile experience of opening it themselves.

- Ask for your customers' impressions before you offer your own. Their first impressions will always be extremely valuable, both to you and to them. Don't trump it with what you think is cool about the home.

- Always start with emotional and dramatic macro statements, and then drill down to the specifics, or micro statements. Customers buy into the big picture first and then validate it with details. It's not in your best interest to begin a discussion of features without first addressing the drama and emotional appeal of the home. Furthermore, when customers try to drag you into the micro details, bring them back to the big picture. ("We'll talk about what's included shortly, but before we do that, let me ask you what you think of the kitchen as a whole.")

- Soft close all along the way. Closing begins in the model demo, so ask lots and lots of minor closes, which I call "anchors." Anchor closes are perfect for use during the demonstration. They're simple, natural, easy, and *critical*. Examples include, "Do you like that?" "Does that work for you?" and, "What do you think of this?" These questions are not complicated, but they are very powerful in getting your customers engaged in the ownership process.

- Sell livability over features. Models are decorated so that prospective buyers can get a visual image of how their family will live in the home. Make sure that this is enhanced by your technique; get them to picture their lives lived out in the room you are showing.

- Close on every room. Be sure that there are no unaddressed concerns before you get to the Plan Close.

- Highlight features that you know your competition does not have. Do NOT mention the competitor by name, but make sure that you point out what your company offers and label that as "one of the distinctives of a quality-built home." Shop your competition!

- Be artistic, passionate, and excited. Elicit emotional responses from the prospects during this emotional process.

- Use the Plan Close. The Plan Close is one of the most powerful moments in the entire transaction. As mentioned previously in this section, when you get a "yes" to the Plan Close, you are well on the way to the sale. Build your entire presentation around this. The best way to get a "yes" is to make sure that the customer has said yes to *every room close.* The best way to a "yes" to every room close is to *use anchors* throughout the whole process. Closing is not a moment; it's a process.

- Immediately transition to a site tour once the plan has been solidified. Don't wait; don't even ask; just go – immediately.

Flora Amir Alikhani, Sales Manager, Portland, Oregon

"To be effective in the model demonstration we focus first on asking prospects how they want to live in the home, and only then pointing out what would work for them. Listening to the prospects and really getting to know them give us the right to come up with creative solutions."

SUMMARY

You simply cannot be great at new home sales if you are not willing to master the art of the demonstration. Further, you'll never be effective in the closing process if you do not demonstrate your models with the closing purpose in mind. The model demonstration and the closing process go hand-in-hand. Want to get good at the closing process? Get into a model home!

In this chapter I've tried to provide both strategy and specific technique, so there should be something in here you can pick up and apply to your own presentation. But if there was one action item I could elevate above all others, it would be this: Start tracking how often you are asking the Plan Close question. Increase the frequency, and you'll increase your sales pace.

THOUGHT-PROVOKERS

1. *Why is the model demonstration even more important in a tough market?*

2. *What do you think is the greatest benefit to a prospect in the model demonstration?*

3. *Is there an area of your presentation that you see that needs work? What specifically can you act on to improve in this area right away?*

Chapter Eight:
Site Like Your Career
Is in the Balance

Salesperson:	*"Can you picture little Johnny riding his tricycle on this driveway?"*
Customer:	*"I can. And it's such a sweet picture. He rides along and gets off the tricycle because I call him in for snacks. And on the way in he knocks over the trash can, and my husband left some motor oil in the can, and it spills into the street and goes into the storm drain, and goes to the river and starts to kill all the little fishies! This is a horrible location!"*
Salesperson:	*"Smokescreen, right? You're saying the lot premium is too high?"*
Customer:	*"Yeh. Did I overplay that a little?"*
Salesperson:	*"A bit, but you get points for creativity."*

I don't think I'll get much disagreement from readers by suggesting that the single biggest difference between a strong market and a tough market lies in the level of customer urgency. In a strong market, prospects carry urgency into the sales offices in buckets. In a challenging market that urgency often feels like it has evaporated into thin air. We can try to build urgency by adding incentives, but that technique has continually proven to be less than effective and horribly expensive.

If there is one aspect of new home sales that fuels urgency more than anything else, it is the practice of siting, or taking potential buyers out for a site tour. For the past twelve years, I have been encouraging salespeople to make this an important part of their routine. In fact, I have challenged literally thousands of new home sales professionals to site more and then watch their sales paces increase. No one has ever returned and reported failure. And there are hundreds of salespeople who have become more successful by implementing this strategy. They site more and track their progress. There is a specific correlation between siting frequency and sales success. Siting is the secret weapon of new home sales. If you get this right, you'll get everything right.

But why is this especially important in a tough market? Siting is so critical because it *creates* urgency. Buyers are faced with the prospect of losing out on something that is truly one-of-a-kind. There is only one Lot 25 at your community, and the customer has the choice of buying it or missing the opportunity. Giving a site tour is the salesperson's single greatest tool for creating urgency, and in a tough market, a successful salesperson needs urgency more than anything else.

Earl Robinson, VP Sales and Marketing, Baltimore, Maryland

"The secret to effective site tours is to focus on 'The ONLY's, thus giving your community separation through uniqueness. For example: 'Happy Acres – This is the ONLY single-family community in Baltimore County with the best schools, standard granite countertops, and ½-acre homesites, all from the $400's.' Make sure you can say at least 4 ONLY's that you have that NO ONE else has."

Siting is also important because it solves a problem that arises with showing models. Model homes are not reality; they are simply representations with which buyers may or may not identify. On the other hand, the site is very real. Customers can touch it, stand on it, and see it. They can envision its potential. They can picture their future lives being lived right on that spot. These sentiments breed emotional urgency, and that is always the most potent form.

Howard Flaschen, Sales Counselor, Jacksonville, Florida

"Whereas before the urgency was built into the market, now there seems to be counter-urgency. Not only are they not in a hurry to buy, but it seems like EVERYTHING is telling them to wait. The media, the price drops, the bigger incentives, the desperation shown in the ads, its all screaming at them to wait and it makes it very difficult to convince them that the home you're demonstrating, the one that they say they love, is the one that they should buy....today. Your greatest weapon is the urgency that comes from getting the customer emotionally attached to just one homesite. The site tour is absolutely critical!"

STOP! DON'T JUST NOD YOUR HEAD!

I know many reading this are probably thinking to themselves, "Yeh, yeh, yeh – siting is important – I get that. Tell me something I haven't heard before." Frankly I am not interested in what you've heard before, nor in what you have learned in training. I am only concerned, as you should be, with what you *do*. Therefore, it is in your best interest to take a moment and really look inside, asking yourself the question, "Do I truly receive the full benefit of my siting opportunities? Is there something I can do immediately to increase both my frequency and effectiveness of site tours?" Do not get caught in the trap of intellectual satisfaction, thinking that you already know about siting. Knowledge is useless without application. Don't ever forget that principle.

*"It is not enough to do your best;
you must know what to do, and THEN do your best."*
W. Edwards Deming

ACTIVITY TRACKING

If you believe in the potential of siting as a means of dramatically increasing your overall sales effectiveness, let's add some specific ideas on how to improve in this area. Activity tracking can be a great way to maximize selling potential. Most new home salespeople only track their weekly traffic, sales, and cancellations, as dictated by their manager. The problem with this strategy is that it doesn't provide much information for analysis. For example, what if a salesperson's traffic count was eighteen, but she only reported one sale? What information is she missing? This salesperson doesn't know what happened to seventeen customers. In a tough market, *all* traffic needs to be accounted for. What happened to the other seventeen visitors?

In order to get your hands around your own efficiency in maximizing every opportunity, start tracking those activities that have the highest chance of ensuring success. You should be tracking not only traffic and sales, but also model demonstrations, pre-qualification conversations, site tours, and closing attempts. In so doing, you can see where your success lies, and also where you can target performance improvement opportunities. For example, if our salesperson from above had reported the following, she would have had something to work with:

- Traffic: 18
- Model demonstrations: 14
- Pre-qualification conversations: 8
- Site tours: 6
- Closing attempts: 6
- Sale: 1

She can now ask some important questions: "Can I improve on the number of pre-qualifications?" "Are the models not showing well?" "If five people did not buy following a closing attempt, do I need to work on my selling skills?" "Do I have a value problem?"

The point of this practice is for you to get analytical about your presentation and about your value equation. Mostly, you can use this technique to track how frequently you get people out on site. Trust me on this – the correlation between site tours and sales written is striking!

FINE POINTS OF SITING

1.   Transitioning from the model home or floor plan

To transition to the site from the model home or floor plan, this is the strongest advice I can offer: *Don't ask - just go!* This should be a salesperson's immediate response to a successful Plan Close (see Chapter Seven). The transition sounds like this:

Salesperson:	*"So, does this look like the right floor plan for you?"*
Buyer:	*"Yes, we really like it."*
Salesperson:	*"Great. I've got two homesites where this plan is being built. Let's take a look and see what you think."*

From this point, the salesperson walks immediately to the site. He doesn't pause and he doesn't ask questions. He just goes. The customer follows his lead because he leads boldly. The salesperson is confident because this is a sale waiting to happen.

2.   Selecting the site

To select the right site for your customers, ask and then listen for clues throughout the sales presentation. Hopefully, they've told you by this point what they're looking for in a homesite, but you need to know that this investigation continues throughout the entire process. The key here is to ask plenty of lifestyle questions. How people live their lives makes a big difference in homesite selection.

Once you know what your customer is looking for, you should have two homesites in mind to show, and you should show the likely lesser choice first. By showing the least probable of the two sites first, you give yourself options. If the buyers like the first site you show, then you're done. If they don't like it, you have a better choice with which to impress them.

3. Preparing a tool kit

To prepare a siting tool kit, consider what you will need to have on hand during the site tour. A successful salesperson will always have the following items in his or her tool kit:

- Blank paper. This is useful for taking notes, writing down questions, and noting reactions.

- Plot plan. Customers will want to know lot dimensions, how the home fits on the lot, setbacks, easements, etc.

- Floor plan. This is especially important when showing sites where the home is not yet under construction. Make sure to pay particular attention to the locations of windows and where they look out on the homesite.

- Hard hats (if required).

- One-hundred-foot measuring tape. This is a great interactive tool for the tour (get your customer holding one end).

- Camera. Take several pictures and email them to the customer. Make sure that the customers are in the picture when you take it!

- "SOLD" stake and hammer. After all, this is the goal!

4. Selling the neighborhood and surrounding areas

To sell the overall community, be prepared to talk about how your customers will live in the area. Remember, people do not just buy the home; they buy the nearby Starbucks, the park, the grocery store, the soccer fields, etc. Furthermore, in a tough market, people specifically look for stability. It is your job to sell the stability of the community.

5. Selling the neighbors

To sell the neighbors, you need entertaining anecdotes at hand about happy, healthy people who are *just like the buyer*. If possible, introduce the buyer to satisfied customers. This is especially important in a tough market. Psychologists tell us that when we make a decision, we become more comfortable with that decision if it is validated by others. Therefore, the residents who have already purchased from you are often your strongest sales force. They can provide the validation that the prospective buyer is looking for. (As a cautionary note, never give out the personal information of your previous customers, including occupation, family size and type, lifestyle, etc.)

6. Selling "livability"

To sell livability you need to demonstrate how your buyers' lives will play out on one specific homesite. Paint a picture for your customers of playing catch in the backyard, pulling into the driveway after a long day's work, or seeing a tricycle left in the front yard. In other words, sell the concept of a "nest." Give your buyer the vision of a home he or she can settle into.

7. Walking the homesite

Walking the site means leaving the sidewalk and getting onto the dirt, and it is important because the site presents different attractions when it is viewed from different perspectives. For example, a homesite looks larger from the back than from the front. In addition, by standing on the two back corners of the lot, the buyer can get an idea of the depth and width of the site.

8.   Asking the "Site Close"

Asking the Site Close question is important because it helps the customer to choose just one location. Remember, salespeople should ask closing questions because these questions benefit the customers; they need to know what works best for them. So, some appropriate closing questions might be, "Could you see yourself pulling into this driveway?" or, "Did I get your location right based on what you've told me about your needs?" Of course, the most essential question is, "Is this the right site?"

The Site Close question is part two of the three-part close. Part one is the Plan Close that was discussed in Chapter Seven. Part two is the Site Close. If you get a "yes" to the closing questions of parts one and two, you are just one Final Close away from landing the sale.

9.   Closing the sale

Without question, the best time and place to close a sale is when you are standing on the homesite. This is the place where you will find emotion and commitment at their highest levels. There is little emotion back in the sales office, so don't take your customers back there to close the sale. Whenever possible (and this should be the majority of the time), ask for the sale while you and the buyers are still on the site. (Chapter Eleven will deal with the methods for asking for a sale in more detail.)

SUMMARY

We are always on the lookout for an urgency advantage, and nowhere will you find a greater urgency-building opportunity than in the site tour. Site more and sell more – it's that simple! You might consider tracking your frequency of site tours and determining whether an increase in site tours leads to an increase in contracts. You might also consider adopting a couple of ideas from this chapter on how to make the site tour more effective by applying new techniques. Most importantly, look for the opportunities to close the sale while you are standing on the site.

THOUGHT-PROVOKERS

1. *Why is the site tour such an important moment in the sales process?*

2. *Are you taking your prospects out on site as much as you can? What could you be doing differently in order to increase your frequency of site demonstrations?*

3. *Could you be more effective in asking for the sale while you are standing on the home site? Do you have a tendency to ask when you're back in the office? Might this be an action item for you – to increase the frequency of final closes while standing on the site?*

Chapter Nine:
Breaking Down Buying Barriers

Salesperson:	*"The kitchen features a very nice…"*
Customer:	*"I object!"*
Salesperson:	*"But I haven't pointed anything out yet."*
Customer:	*"Sorry – I'm just warming up. Go ahead"*
Salesperson:	*"The kitchen."*
Customer:	*"It's overpriced! Overpriced, I say!"*
Salesperson:	*"This is going to take a while."*
Customer:	*"I object to that assessment!"*

"The problem that is located and identified is already half-solved."

Bror R. Carlson

CHAPTER NINE: HELPING TO BREAK DOWN BARRIERS

Your homes may be described by your customers in many flattering ways. They may be described as "spacious," "attractive," or "well-designed." However, one of the words that will never be used to describe your homes is "perfect." I know this without even looking at the homes you are selling because I know this important principle: *There is no such thing as a perfect home.* When purchasing a new home, everyone compromises. You, me, Bill Gates . . . everyone. There is nothing wrong with compromising and buying a less-than-perfect home. In fact, it is a very normal occurrence.

Buyers compromise on aspects of homes as long as the perceived negatives are not deal-killers. For example, they may not like the busy street, but they'll put up with it. Or, they want a three-car garage, but they'll take a two-car. They'd love to have granite slab, but they'll accept granite tile. For these customers, the busy street, the two-car garage, and the granite tile are not deal-killers. They're aspects of the home that they will have to put up with, and they are willing to do so.

Because everyone compromises when buying a new home, there is a certain level of dissatisfaction that accompanies the purchase. Therefore, a necessary and critical objective in the sales process is determining the buyer's acceptable level of dissatisfaction. For example, there are more than a million new homes built every year in the United States. Plenty of these homes are affected by the presence of power lines. However, people still buy these homes. They don't do so because they love power lines. They buy because this particular aspect of the home falls under the category of "acceptable level of dissatisfaction" for them.

There is no such thing as a perfect home, and every buyer on the planet needs to come to this realization and justify the purchase of a less-than-perfect home. But be aware that this process is made more difficult in tough market conditions.

Dan Koontz, VP Sales, Fresno, California

"The skill of overcoming objections distinguishes the amateur from the professional sales associate. In today's market, it is the difference between making and losing the sale."

OBJECTIONS IN A TOUGH MARKET

One characteristic of a tough market is a larger supply of homes and, thus, more choices for the buyer. More choices make for a more difficult buying process because there are more options that need to be eliminated. Because homebuyers are offered more choices, they broaden the factors by which they eliminate these options. These eliminating factors are the "deal-killers" we just spoke of. Salespeople need to do as much as possible to eliminate the deal-killers that are in their control in order to sell their homes.

For example, in a strong market, the salesperson's attitude is not necessarily a deal-killer. In a tough market, it's all the customer needs to eliminate that entire community as an option and walk away from the deal. Similarly, in a strong market, tattered flags or wilting flowers are not a big deal, but in a tough market, these things portend a lack of attention to detail, and this becomes a deal-killer.

OBJECTIONS AS BUYING SIGNALS

Consider the two following scenarios:

Scenario 1: A customer comes into your office, but you're busy with another buyer, so she goes to the model by herself. While she's there, she finds something that is a deal-killer for her. She comes back through the sales office and can't wait to get out. There's nothing that you can do to convince her to stay.

Scenario 2: A customer comes into your office, but you're busy with another buyer, so he goes to the model by himself. While he's there, he finds something that he perceives to be a problem – let's say railroad tracks. He comes back into your office with an anguished look on his face. He says, "Oh man, those railroad tracks are so close by. That's a problem."

In the first scenario, the problem that the woman finds is truly a deal-killer. Customers who find deal-killers don't stand around and describe them to you. They just leave.

In the second scenario, the problem that the man finds might just fall under his level of acceptable dissatisfaction. This is obvious for one reason: *because he hasn't left.* If the railroad tracks were a deal-killer, he would have been gone just like the woman in the first scenario. If he doesn't leave, you can assume that the railroad tracks are a problem, but not a deal-killer. The customer is giving you a chance, and what he really is saying is,

> *"I don't like the railroad tracks at all, but I like everything else, and I might need to accept the railroad tracks. This is something that I might consider within my acceptable level of dissatisfaction, but I need your help. Give me some assurance that this is a good thing to do."*

The message this customer is sending you is, "Help me!" He wants to consider moving to the next step, but he needs your help to get there. The next move is yours.

When customers raise objections, they are telling the salesperson two things. First, they are saying, "I'm not comfortable with this compromise, and I need to talk through it with someone." And, secondly, they are saying, "I trust you to help me." In other words, the raising of objections by a customer is a powerful buying sign. The salesperson shouldn't panic; he should be excited. He has three powerful phrases at his disposal: "Talk to me," "Tell me what concerns you," and "I understand – let's talk about it."

> ## Jim Suth, Sales Trainer, Danville, California
>
> *"OK. So the market is tough. You can't pretend you don't read the paper! What you need to do to stay focused is to change your mindset. The toughest objection to overcome at your community might be <u>your</u> memory of "how it used to be". You need to completely erase the past and start fresh. This weekend you need to have a Grand Opening! Remember how you acted when you were first opening? You fretted over the price sheets. You started getting ready for Saturday on Wednesday. You blew the balloons up yourself. On Saturday the day of the Grand Opening you were actually early! Start over, especially to rewire your brain. Have a Grand Opening this weekend!"*

FOUR STEPS TO HANDLING BUYER OBJECTIONS

1. Don't jump to conclusions.

Jumping to conclusions is the most serious *and* most common violation of good selling technique. Salespeople have a natural tendency to internalize their own objections, and then they project these objections onto their customers. The customer is therefore assumed to have the objections that the salesperson has internalized.

Of course, this is a mistake; when a salesperson allows his own biases to influence the sales conversation, he ends up increasing buyer anxiety. Consider the aforementioned issue of power lines. Power lines are considered undesirable because of three main reasons: aesthetics, health, or resale value. After polling people around the country, I have found that the three objections are evenly spread among new home sales professionals. In other words, about one-third of those polled objected to power lines on the basis of aesthetics; one-third objected on the basis of health; and one-third objected on the basis of resale value. If a salesperson projects his own personal basis for the objection onto the buyer, he will be out of sync with the buyer's concern two-thirds of the time. This will result in the salesperson bringing up an objection that the customer never had considered!

This is how this interaction would look:

Customer:	*"I'm really concerned about the power lines."*
Salesperson:	*"I understand. But we've got all kinds of literature from the utility company regarding potential health concerns from EMF's emitted from the lines. You actually have more health danger from your microwave oven or your hair dryer."*
Customer:	*"Did you say health concerns? I just thought that they were ugly."*

This salesperson has given a second concern or anxiety to the buyer without even addressing the principal issue. In a tough market, buyers are looking to eliminate; they are seeking out deal-killers. The last thing a salesperson should do is add his or her own personal biases to those concerns that the buyer has already adopted.

2. Question the objection to make sure that you're clear.

After allowing the customer to talk, a salesperson should re-question and re-phrase. Having an accurate understanding of the objection is imperative. A wrong understanding could lead to the introduction of another objection by the salesperson.

Here are some sample questions:

- "Okay, you're worried that the proximity to industrial areas might hurt your resale value. Do I have that right?"

- "So your primary concern is that the schools may not be up to par. Is that correct?"

- "I hear you saying that the lot size is too small for a pool, but that otherwise you are okay with the homesite. Is that right?"

3. Answer the objection by providing a positive counterbalance.

There are hundreds of different objections that buyers can present to salespeople and scores of possible answers to each objection. The purpose of this book is not to outline all the possible responses for every objection (that would be one LONG book!). However, top sales-people have answers prepared for the objections that they encounter most frequently. Therefore, to become a more effective salesperson, you should list your most frequent objections and come up with answers to them. Good sources of possible answers are peers, previous customers who have dealt with similar objections, and Realtors.

To answer the objection, you must not attempt to eliminate it. Not only is this impossible, but it seeks to invalidate the customer's opinion. The objective of answering the objection is to *neutralize* it. Neutralizing a negative is best accomplished by introducing a positive. To neutralize a buyer's objection, find a positive counterbalance that puts a positive spin on the buyer's concern.

Neutralizing even the most complicated objections can often be very simple. The buying process is like a weighted scale. For example, on one side of the scale, the home looks great on many levels. On the other, it has the highest assessments in town. Those high assessments will not go away or change; that is, you cannot eliminate that objection. They need to be counteracted by something – they need a positive counterbalance.

An appropriate reply intended to even out the scale might sound like the following: "It's true that the assessments are higher than in other communities in the area, but remember that you are making a decision based on all of the information presented to you, not on just one factor. While the assessments are higher, I'm sure that you'll agree that the master-planned community is absolutely beautiful, more so than any other in the area. In addition, the assessments fund the long-term upkeep of the community, so it protects your future resale value."

Of course, this response does not eliminate the objection, but the objective here is not to eliminate. The goal is only to neutralize. Hope-fully, this reply will give the buyer a sufficiently positive perspective to neutralize the issue.

The Power of Positive Rationalizations

Consider this scenario: You're in Nordstrom. You see a pair of shoes that cost $250.00. You love the shoes and want to buy them, but you have a price objection.

What you need most at this moment is, surprisingly, not $250.00. In fact, what you really need more than anything else is a big juicy rationalization. If you can justify the cost, you'll find the money. All people go through this rationalization process throughout the course of the day. Because rationalization is subconscious and powerful, humans can justify almost anything when necessary.

Because there is no such thing as a perfect home, the customer needs to rationalize acceptance of its negative aspects. *This is a process that every single homebuyer undergoes every time a home is purchased.*

To make yourself more adept at handling objections, try the following two activities. First, take objections like railroad tracks, flight paths, small bedrooms, or small backyards, and think of positive counterbalances for each. Second, bring up these objections at your sales meetings and ask your peers for counterbalance ideas. They may give you some new thoughts to use in your sales presentation.

Sometimes simple rationalizations are all the motivation that the buyer needs to make a decision. Don't think of your suggestions for rationalizations as manipulation. Remember that buyers create their own rationalizations all the time, and your suggestions are simply helping with a very normal process.

4. Confirm that the objection has been neutralized.

Once an objection has been addressed, it is critical that the salesperson asks for confirmation. He or she must ensure that the customer agrees that the objection has been neutralized. If the customer has not confirmed his or her acceptance of the objectionable aspect of the home, the issue may arise again. Often unsettled objections are reasserted at the close with unfavorable results.

Sample confirmation prompts are:

- "Did we get that taken care of?"
- "Is this something that you can live with?"
- "I know it's not the perfect answer, and there is no such thing as a perfect purchase, but on the whole do we have a workable situation here?"
- "Is this something that you're willing to accept? Can we move on?"

When you have confirmed that the objection has been neutralized, move on! There is no need to dwell on the subject for one more moment. Change the subject and advance the sale to the next level. If you're not sure where to go when the objection has been neutralized, try asking a closing question!

Dan Koontz, VP Sales, Fresno, California

"Our customers come to us with concerns and objections. In their hearts they want to buy a new home. They desperately want and need for us to overcome their objections. All too often we forget that we are the experts in the home sales process. We must not forget that our experience and training prepares us to be problem solvers. And, our sales success depends on our ability to seek out the customer's issues and to put to rest their concerns."

THE COMPETITION'S OBJECTIONS

One final recommendation is that salespeople should become keenly aware of the objections to their competitors' homes. In a tough market where people are looking to eliminate options, buyers are deciding which objections carry the most weight. While salespeople should never bash a competitor, especially by name, they should understand what the drawbacks of that competitor's homes are. This gives greater selling leverage and more information with which to neutralize objections.

Should a customer bring up another community in the conversation, particularly if the competing community has higher incentives or a lower price, it is appropriate to point out the benefits that you offer by leveraging off of the competitions negatives. For example:

- "That is a fine community. Of course, we offer a much quieter community because we do not back up to the freeway."

- "You can pay less if you are willing to compromise on the lot size. But if you want the 6,000 square foot lot this is the community for you."

- "Others might have higher incentives, but they also have higher assessments. You'll be paying for those higher incentives for years."

SUMMARY

There is no such thing as a perfect home, and the homebuying prospect must go through the process of determining where they are willing to compromise. The voicing of this concern comes out in the form of an objection. Top performers embrace objections as a natural part of the buying cycle. They understand that their prospect is sending out a call for help, and they are prepared to aid the customer through this important part of the decision-making process.

THOUGHT-PROVOKERS

1. *Do certain objections sometimes scare you? If so, why?*

2. *If you saw the objection as a buying sign rather than a complaint, might that mindset make you a more effective sales counselor?*

3. *Are there common objections in your community to which you would benefit from having planned your response in advance? Can you think up some positive counterbalances for these objections?*

4. *Might you be guilty of planting negative thoughts in the minds of your customers based on your own perceived objections?*

Chapter Ten:
Selling to the Relentless Deal-Maker

Husband:	*"I'm gonna get the deal of a lifetime. They're asking $500,000 – I'm getting this house for $410,000!"*
Wife:	*"Harold, you always say that, and then you fold like an envelope.."*
Husband:	*"Watch me! Hey buddy, I'm offering $410,000 for this house and I ain't paying a dime more than that."*
Salesperson:	*"No problem. I've got one at that price, but you don't get the expanded garage or the game room or the pool. And of course we can't offer the big-screen plasma TV promotion at that price. Shall we write it up?"*
Husband:	*"Heh, heh. I was just kidding. Can you make it $510,000?"*

Let me throw one opinion out there right away. It's controversial. It flies directly in the face of a standard practice in our industry, especially in a tough market. You might not agree with me. Just hear me out and give it some thought.

I submit to you that four of the most difficult words for the home-buying customer to hear are these: "Make me an offer!" I believe there are few phrases that both confuse the buyer's value equation and demonstrate builder desperation as much as this one.

Let me give you some context to this argument. Let's suppose you have a neighbor who has fallen on hard times. He's looking to sell some of his personal effects to pay his bills. He shows you his original Leroy Neiman drawing of Muhammad Ali from 1975. He assures you that the print is very valuable and that it will continue to appreciate, and you believe him. Because he is desperate, he is willing to sell the print at a low price. Then he says, "Make me an offer!"

That's the scenario. Assuming that you have an interest, either for your own collection or as an investment, what are you going to offer? For the purpose of illustration, I want you to come up with a number in your head right now. Do you have one?

I've asked this question in training sessions, and I've heard everything from one dollar to one thousand dollars, but rarely does anyone come close to the actual appraised price of $9,000. Why do people offer so low a price? It's simple – because they have no idea what the true value is.

The reality is that customers do not wish to pay one dollar more than they need to. So when we invite them to "make an offer," we are asking for a lowball offer. And we get these offers not because prospects are unethical slimeballs, but because they honestly don't know where the bottom of the market is until they get rejected and start moving up. The very words "make me an offer" put the prospects in a position where they must attack the value proposition.

The truth is that some homebuyers are fine with getting a good price, but many aren't content until they believe they've received the very best terms available. How do they get these terms? By pressing and pressing and pressing even further. Consider this pressure to be a test. The customer wants to know where the limits are. He wants to know he is getting the best possible deal. He wants to push the envelope whenever he can. But you need to keep in mind that your company is doing *exactly the same thing.* There is no law that mandates our sales prices. As salespeople, we are trying to get top dollar for our homes at all times. We put a price out there that we believe is not one penny less than market value. We all want the best terms; that's the nature of any sales transaction.

What, then, should you say to a prospect when it comes time to put something on paper? Try, "Let me help you craft an offer." This phrasing is far less scary to a prospect, as it implies that you have a partnership with your future homeowner.

Tough markets call for new home sales professionals to hone their negotiation skills. Here are some suggestions for dealing with this deal-driven homebuyer:

Rich Ambrosini, Homebuilding Division President, Concord, California

"You have to understand the context in which the offer has been presented. How real is this buyer? Are they just fishing, or are they really motivated, and for the right reason? We cannot allow ourselves to be bullied by low-ball offers — the offer has to be based on some inherent value. After all, who is the industry expert – is it us or is it them?"

"Let us never negotiate out of fear, but let us never fear to negotiate."
John F. Kennedy

1. Understand the Perspective.

In the end, this prospective buyer simply wants to know that he got the best deal that he could get and that there was not a single dollar left on the table. As everyone knows, the fear of overlooking anything can be overwhelming. In fact, when the customer believes that he could have received more out of the deal, he will likely reopen negotiations after the fact to satisfy this disturbing curiosity.

The customer isn't wrong for having these very human concerns, and he isn't a jerk for asking for everything. He is the buyer, and while he might cause us some frustration through his persistent badgering, we are in no position to offer a moral judgment on his character.

Before turning to a hasty and negative reaction, take a moment to try to see things from the customer's perspective. Ask yourself some important questions:

- "Do I have a strong sense of where this customer is coming from?"
- "Have I sought to put myself in his shoes?"
- "Is this customer convinced of the value in the home, or do I have more work to do in that area?"
- "Is there a competitor who is "training" the customer to ask for more?"
- "Have I done something to indicate that we will, in fact, move on the price?"
- "Am I firmly convinced in the value of the offering?"

As you can see, these questions encourage you to consider more carefully the customer's position.

There is one other important aspect to considering the customer's position. In many cultures negotiation is a way of life. This is neither good nor bad – it simply *is*. If a person is accustomed to negotiating over the price of a melon at the market, wouldn't it stand to reason that he would want to negotiate over the price of a home? There are customers who are incredulous when they are told that the price of a home is non-negotiable. One customer I had simply refused to believe me when I told him we would not negotiate; he even accused me of lying. Eventually I turned him over to my sales manager, who confirmed my position. At the end of the conversation he was furious, and he stormed out of my office. My guess is that he bought a different home from someone who was willing to negotiate with him. He bought the best deal, but not necessarily the best value.

For customers whose cultures operate upon negotiation, you might need to offer a (very sensitive) education if you are not in that type of selling situation: "You might be used to negotiating the terms in the purchase of a home; in some areas [note that I said "areas," not "cultures" or "countries"] it is quite common. However, here the best price you will ever get is what you've already been quoted. That might not be consistent with your experience, but that's the way we do it at this community. And you can be assured that you are getting the very best term available.

Jeff Miles, Regional VP, Sales, Newport Beach, California

"Today's buyers often negotiate from a sense of fear. A sales counselor's job is to affirm the reasons they are buying a home and establish the value in what they have to offer, before true negotiation can begin."

---

2. Find the win-win.

Too frequently salespeople find themselves on the defense, impatiently waiting for customers to finish their point, so that they can jump in with an explanation of why they are about to say "no." This scenario is a classic manifestation of an "I win, you lose" approach to sales. Fortunately, it doesn't have to be that way. As a salesperson, you should always be looking for middle ground. Let prospective buyers know that you desire to help them as long as they are willing to understand the company's position as well: "You want the best terms you can get, and I appreciate that. You are aware, I'm sure, that the company has interests that need to be protected as well. So what I want to do is find a solution that works best for both of us. Let's start with a discussion about what is most important to you and why."

Notice that the final sentence of that statement suggests a new direction for the conversation. When you can get a customer talking, you can open the lines of communication and obtain a more thorough understanding of his or her point of view and values. From there you can strategize as to where to take the conversation.

For further quality reading on this subject, I recommend Leigh Steinberg's excellent book, *Winning With Integrity: Getting What You Want Without Selling Your Soul*. This is an outstanding book on negotiating written by one of the world's most prominent negotiators. Steinberg's premise is that understanding the person with whom you are working is the key to success in negotiations.

> *"Negotiators with a fixed-pie bias assume that for them to win something, the other side must lose it."*
> **Max Bazerman**

3. Don't Focus on the "Best Price."

Stay away from discussions about the "best price." Labeling something as "my best price" is hackneyed and therefore not credible. My longtime mentor, Lisa Kalmbach, taught me that vigorous shoppers are not really looking for the best price. The customer really wants to know the salesperson's *last* price. In essence, the customer is saying, "I am looking for the point where you are absolutely done, where if I asked for one dollar more, you would turn me down and allow me to walk away." This is the last price, and using this term brings comfort to the customer who often needs nothing more than to know that there was not one dollar left on the table.

A last price response might sound like this: "I appreciate your wanting the best terms you can get, and I respect that. But you need to understand that the price I've given you is not only my best price, but also it is my last *price*. You need to make a decision as to whether there is enough value in this home to justify this price."

4. Threaten the Takeaway.

Because deal-driven customers are often consumed with getting the possible deal, they find themselves absorbed in a rational analysis of terms, and they forget the very emotional reasons for which they fell in love with the home in the first place. When customers neglect and ignore their emotions regarding a home, these emotions diminish. As a salesperson, you need to do everything in your power to keep that from happening. The customers need to remain emotionally engaged. You need to keep them emotionally charged over the purchase of their dream home and then threaten to sell it to someone else if the terms cannot be agreed upon.

In other words, sometimes all a customer needs to know is that you are preparing to sell the home (their dream home) to someone else. Don't be afraid to be direct with the takeaway: "Mr. Williams, it does not appear that you love this home enough and that you are having a hard time justifying the price. Perhaps you need to be looking at something else. It might be time to throw in the towel on this one." Of course, this is risky. Mr. Williams could, after all, walk away. However, it does tend to stir people to action.

> *"True luck consists not in holding the best of the cards at the table; Luckiest he who knows just when to rise and go home."*
> **John Hay**

NEGOTIATION TIPS

When it is time to negotiate an offer, consider these tips and techniques:

1. Don't negotiate in hypotheticals. Do not bother asking your sales manager about where the bottom line price is until you have a signed offer in hand. As a sales counselor, I'm not interested in what the prospect might do if we come down far enough on the price. If a customer wants a better price, he must ask me on paper.

    There is something that implies commitment when writing a check and signing a contract, even if it is only an offer to purchase. You need every bit of commitment that you can muster at this point. The conversation sounds like this: "My boss wants to know that you are serious, and you are serious when you actually write an offer. Let's put that on paper."

2. Prepare the prospect for a counter-offer, even before you present the original offer. If you simply say to the customer, "I'll see what I can do," you are leaving the prospect with the idea that there is a good chance that the offer will be accepted. From that perspective, the prospect is now set on the offered price and will be sorely disappointed when a counter-offer comes in. In other words, the customer is locked into a simple thumbs up or thumbs down position; if the deal is accepted they buy and if it is rejected or countered they walk.

    Your response to an offer may sound like this: "I have a good sense of what the company is willing to take, based on past sales. Your offer is low, and that's okay – you always want to be aggressive on these things. I believe the counter-offer will come in between x and y, and if it does, that's still a great value, don't you think?" Notice that I asked a closing question on the counter price. You'll want to do that even before you present the original offer.

3. Counter with an odd number. Ask your sales manager to come up with some kind of formula so that the counter-offer is a calculated number, not a number that was clearly pulled out of thin air. If the original offer is for $325,000 and the counter would normally come in at $340,000, ask the sales manager to counter with $342,640. This implies that there was a formula followed to get to this number.

4. Present the counter with enthusiasm. Let the prospect know that he or she is getting an excellent price. Your best bet is to present the counter as if the sale is a done deal. Present with the assumption that the prospect will sign off on the countered price.

Tracy Miller, Sales Trainer, Jacksonville, Florida (tmillersales@gmail.com)

"Always begin with a great presentation that centers around finding the best home for them. If you were to ask them to tell you the exact monthly payment or rent payment of the last five places they lived, they would only be able to give you a ballpark figure at best. But if you asked them to describe in detail every room in the last five places they lived, they would be able to do it. Remind them of that. Again, find a home that fits their needs, get them excited about it and then close them with an incentive that makes them feel as though they got a good deal."

SUMMARY

Salespeople have the responsibility to diligently respect and defend the value propositions of the homes they sell, even in the face of pressure. Top performers have this characteristic – they don't get dragged into the muck by those with little respect for the value of their homes. But they are also adept at negotiating with prospects to ensure win-win outcomes.

My friends, stick to your guns and stick to your value proposition. Your customers want and need you to demonstrate that the homes they are about to buy are worth the price they are about to pay. You are, in fact, doing a tremendous service to your customer when you are diligent in defending your value.

THOUGHT-PROVOKERS

1. *Do you sometimes find yourself getting "freaked out" when a customer wants to make an offer? Would practice in this area make you more confident?*

2. *Do you really believe strongly enough in your own value to defend it in a contract negotiation? Perhaps you have some "self-selling" to do.*

3. *What mindsets, tips, or techniques from this chapter would make you a better negotiator? What action plans can you put in place?*

Chapter Eleven:
Ask and Ask and Ask Again

Sales Manager:	*"You must ask the closing question at least five times?"*
Salesperson:	*"Okay. Got it. By the way, can I have Saturday off?"*
Sales Manager:	*"Are you kidding me? Of course not!"*
Salesperson:	*"Okay. Well then can I have Saturday off?"*
Sales Manager:	*"I said no! Are you deaf?"*
Salesperson:	*"No, but can I have Saturday off?"*
Sales Manager:	*"Okay, I get it – that's cute. You're mocking me, aren't you?"*
Salesperson:	*"Heavens no. Wouldn't dream of it. Can I have Saturday off?"*

"Put that coffee down! Coffee is for closers!"
Alec Baldwin, Glengarry Glen Ross

Somehow, in the field of new home sales, asking for the sale – closing – has become something of a lost art. Typically, a strong market does not require the salesperson to do the asking; the customers ask the salespeople if they can buy! When the market suddenly changes, the art of closing becomes necessary, but salespeople find that this skill has become weak with lack of use.

Joanne Williams, Owner, J. Williams Staffing, Irvine, California

"If a salesperson is paralyzed with fear and discomfort when 'asking for the check,' they really must have a frank conversation with themselves regarding their willingness to change old habits and their mindset. This market will definitely sort the real closers from the rest of the bunch! Moreover, they will be the most sought-after agents when the market returns primarily because of their experience, adaptability, and strength."

For salespeople, the objective of the job is to get sales – period. And he who does not ask will not receive. Top performers have this in common – they are outstanding when it comes to closing the sale.

To treat this topic thoroughly, I want to talk briefly about what I often refer to in training as the "yielder" tendencies of many salespeople, those times when we face discomfort and yield; that is, when we take the easy and more comfortable path. This tendency to avoid discomfort (which leads to yielding moments) is masked in a strong market, but the tough market exposes the yielders for who they are. The salesperson who yields to discomfort is looking for the easy road. And the longer the closing skills go unused the more the yielder instincts have a tendency to spread.

The danger of this behavior becomes clear, of course, when a yielding salesperson meets a yielding homebuyer. They'll become best friends, but there ain't gonna be no sale! Ironically, the yielder then makes up a story that goes something like, "I don't want to make this person uncomfortable, so I won't ask for the sale. I'll wait for him to let me know when he's ready." Talk about high-pressure sales! Forcing your customer to come to you, hat in hand, and humbly ask you for permission to buy???? That's high-pressure sales at its absolute worst!

We must re-visit the topic of sales as a service we provide to our customers. When viewed from this perspective, there is no disrespect in asking a closing question. Once again, it should be clear that these strategies are not manipulations. They are methods for helping the customer get what he or she wants. To do this, the salesperson must fight the yielding tendency, be bold, and *ask for the sale.*

Before outlining strategies for asking, we must begin with two basic premises for this discussion. First, closing is a process; it is not a single moment. Second, closing is something done for the benefit of the customer, not the salesperson.

CLOSING AS A PROCESS

Too often, the close is seen as a single culminating moment at the end of the sales discussion. In truth, top performers understand that success comes by asking closing questions early and continuing to close throughout the sale. It is the weak salesperson that views the close as one gigantic question, the answer to which either seals or de-stroys the deal. Actually, there is no one end-all question, no such holy grail for the salesperson to seek. Closing is not a specific moment; it is a process that begins early and continues throughout.

Closing should be thought of as a bridge. At the beginning of the sales process, it's like the sale is on one side of a wide canyon and the salesperson and the customer are on the other. Each closing question builds part of a bridge between the sides. It would take an incredible question to get from one side to the other in one closing attempt. But the idea of closing as a process says that each small closing question along the way could add a plank to the bridge. By the time the process is finished, the final closing question is simple and natural, a logical conclusion to the presentation.

> ## Barbara Moczulski, Sales Counselor, Mission Viejo, California
>
> *"The purpose of the closing questions is to take those 'baby steps' that eventually lead you to a successful sale. You need to obtain critical information with regards to the family needs and time frame and set goals to the time frames with regards to what you have available, standing inventory, pre-sales etc. All this information works together when it's time to ask for the sale."*

CLOSING FOR THE CUSTOMER'S BENEFIT

If closing is manipulation, then it becomes a burden. We cannot pretend to love our customers and seek to serve their best interests and then attempt to use an "old-school" trick close to get them to purchase. Unfortunately, much of the tripe that has been passed off as legitimate technique has preached an approach that is quite the opposite of legitimate.

I'll quote here from the introduction to a book on closing techniques that you can find in almost any book store in the United States: "This book is a straightforward, honest discussion of proven tricks and traps that produce sales." There is not even a hint of shame that the book is about tricking people. Small wonder then that many of the actual closing attempts are described as follows:

- "This close is intended to embarrass and control the customer, and it does just that."

- "In this close, the closer throws the customer's objection right back at him and makes him eat his own words."

- "This close is intended to embarrass and shame the customer into buying."

- "When using this close, the customer will feel like an idiot and go ahead and purchase."

The biggest problem with this kind of garbage is not what it does to the customer but rather how it plays on the psyche of the sales professional. When we begin to believe that closing equals manipulation, we will never be able to offer our customers effective service.

But if closing is something that the salesperson does *for* the customer instead of *to* the customer, closing becomes a valuable part of the service provided. This should be precisely the case. Closing questions are asked for the customer's benefit. They help buyers verify their own values. For example, let's say that a salesperson asks the customer a kitchen close question ("So, is this the kitchen you were hoping to find?"). Is this question more valuable because it confirms value in the mind of the salesperson or because it confirms value in the mind of the buyer? Do you see where we are headed with this? I don't ask the kitchen close question because I want to know whether the kitchen works. I ask the question so that the *customer* can come to grips with whether the kitchen works. Every closing question helps the buyer to understand another piece of the value puzzle.

This perspective often becomes skewed, and salespeople view closing as disrespectful (that's the yielder in them talking). Their logic says, "The customer will let me know when he's ready to buy." While this is true for some buyers, it's not true for most buyers. For the customers who don't speak up, it is disrespectful to *not close*. This forces a customer to ask your permission to buy one of your homes and puts a great deal of pressure on them. While the close must be done respectfully and professionally, it is something that is owed to customers, so don't make them ask. Ask them!

Barbara Moczulski, Sales Counselor, Mission Viejo, California

"I ask every time, 'Do you want to buy this house?' If you don't ask, the next salesperson they meet will ask and they will get the sale, not you. My feeling is if I am going to site, give out payments, demonstrate . . . I want to be rewarded for my hard work!"

CLOSING IN A TOUGH MARKET

As new home professionals, we are looking for every possible advantage to deal with tough market conditions. But then, the sales process isn't about us, now is it? Of course not. The sales process is about serving our customers' best interests.

Strong markets are noteworthy for the confidence that buyers have in making a purchase decision. Asking a salesperson for permission to buy a home becomes simple and even necessary when the inventory is short and the momentum is strong. Prospects have the strong hope of twenty-percent appreciation rates to alleviate any fears they might have.

In a challenging market, fear is rampant, and the customer, faced with far too many choices in the search, must eliminate options all along the way. One way for customers to eliminate is to avoid accepting value in a home. This happens every time they evaluate a home through purely logical eyes, without really considering how they might live their lives in the home. But in a challenging market, the strong salesperson who asks plenty of closing questions will cause prospects to *ask themselves* whether value is established, whether the home meets their needs, and in fact whether they are truly in love with what they are seeing. Don't expect a nervous buyer to get emotionally tied to a home if you refuse to ask closing questions!

Now let's examine some of the different types of closing questions that are commonly asked in the sales process.

CONFIRMATION CLOSES

Confirmation closes are called many things including "tie-downs" or "anchors." These closes are the small and natural confirmations of value throughout the sales process, and they are crucial.

Throughout a sale, confirmation closes secure value in many aspects of the home along the way, but they also do something even more important by engaging the prospective buyer. Every time a top performer asks a confirmation close, she gets something important in return: engagement. She gets the customer involved in defining his or her own version of value. If a salesperson never asks these minor closing questions, she leaves value up in the air.

Think about a really simple confirmation close, something like, "Do you like this?" This question is neither complex nor manipulative. It is, in fact, entirely conversational. Why is it important, and what does the question elicit? It brings about the active and meditative involvement of the prospect. It forces the customer to say, "Yes, I like this," or "No, I don't." Either way, we advance the sale on a deeper level.

Confirmation closes are particularly important in a tough market. Selling in a challenged market calls for increased customer involvement. In this scenario, the salesperson can't wait for a customer to initiate the purchase, and he can't wait for customers to generate their own excitement and energy. He must ask the questions that get customers involved and committed.

Before we move on, we must discuss a significant risk. My fear is that many will read the preceding paragraphs and say, "I already know that. They go over 'tie-downs' in Sales 101." That's true. But I'm not interested in whether you know it. I'm only interested in whether you do it! There is a major difference between knowing and doing, and success comes from the latter. There are scores of salespeople that could get a 100% mark on a test about closing theory, but the successful salespeople are the ones who actually put the techniques into play. I beg you

– take some evaluative time and determine whether you are truly using confirmation closes to your greatest advantage.

THE ROOM CLOSE

The Room Close question is very simple: "Does this room work for you?" As a salesperson, you should have a goal in mind every time you enter into a room during the model demo – to ask the Room Close question before you leave. It's short and sweet, but very important. Again, this question is critical because it is asked for the customer's best interest. It involves the prospect in the process of determining his or her sense of value.

The Room Close does not require much technique; frankly, it's not that hard. In fact, anyone can ask the question. However, few salespeople actually do practice the Room Close, mostly because it is not about technique, but about mindset and strategy. Salespeople who don't use the Room Close don't understand its power. Remember we have said that closing is a process, not a moment in time. The next step in the process – the Plan Close – is one of the most critical steps in the entire closing sequence, and it is set up beautifully with a series of Room Close questions.

To see the power of the Room Close, try focusing for a time only on the Room Close and the Plan Close questions during your demo. Make this a top priority; begin to practice it with every demo; make it part of your routine. You'll see dramatic results. And if the customer says yes to every Room Close, it provides the perfect segue into the all-important Plan Close question.

THE PLAN CLOSE

The Plan Close question was addressed in Chapter Seven, but it is such an important part of the closing process that it bears repeating, hopefully leading to a deeper understanding of this concept.

The Plan Close question, like most closing questions, is very simple: "Does this floorplan work for you?" But if it is really that simple, what makes it so powerful? Just consider that the entire sales presentation can be anchored by this one question! The Plan Close question is so critical because when the buyer says yes, she is telling the salesperson that she accepts the plan . . . and the price . . . and the location . . . and everything else that's been discussed up until this point in the sale. Moreover, when she agrees to the floorplan, it is easy to jump right into the site tour and the subsequent sale.

The Plan Close can be an incredibly effective anchor for your sale. Build your process to lead up to this question, and drive to the finish line once the question has been asked. You might consider setting a target this weekend for how many times you can ask the Plan Close question. Set a goal and keep track. You'll find that your sales pace can be directly affected by the frequent use of this potent close.

To effectively use the Plan Close, make it a specific and memorable step for the customer. Stop at the front door, turn around, and say, "Before we leave, did we find the right floor plan for you?" That's it! Resist the urge to make this question any more difficult than it needs to be. Just remember that you are not asking for your own benefit, but for that of the homebuyer. If the buyer has affirmed in his or her own mind that this is the right plan, the next step is obvious – let's go look at homesites!

THE CHECK-IN CLOSE

Ever get to the point in the sale when you're just not sure where you're at with the prospect? Ever find an awkward pause in the discussion? The Check-In Close is made for these situations. This closing question is asked for the salesperson's benefit, and it answers the question, "Where am I in the process?" When posed to the customer, Check-In Closes sound like these questions:

- "Tell me what you're thinking."

- "I know this can all be a bit overwhelming. Is there anything that concerns you right now?"

- "Are you having fun?"

- "Do you have any questions at this point in the process?

- "Do you like what you see so far?"

These questions are great to insert from time to time into the sales conversation, during potentially uncomfortable moments like the walk to the homesite. They are simple and natural, and they give you an immediate understanding of how the prospect is doing.

The Check-In Close is also a powerful antidote to the awkward pause, which can be sale-threatening. While it is true that a salesperson who talks too much is sure to endanger the sale, the opposite situation (silence) can be equally dangerous. When there is too much silence, the customer begins to feel that the responsibility lies on his shoulders to lead the conversation. That's a lot of pressure on a customer, especially in a tough market where he is already unsettled. We always want to take the lead in the sales process, and we do this most effectively by asking questions.

THE SITE CLOSE

If a buyer agrees to go to the site with you, she is sending you a very powerful message: that she is close to a decision! Your customer knows how the game is played. Once you find a plan she likes, the very next step is to find the right homesite. After that there are no major decisions left in the process.

Therefore, whenever you go out on site, you should *always* be thinking about the final close. Whenever possible, it's best to close while standing with the buyer on the site. While this is good advice in any market, it's especially valuable in a tough market. In challenging sales environments salespeople need urgency, more than anything else, on their side, and the site tour is one of the few urgency opportunities they have at their disposal.

The Site Close is a perfect and natural set-up to the Final Close. The Site Close, like the Plan Close question, is not difficult: "Did we find the right homesite for you?" or "Out of the locations you've seen, does this one seem to fit your needs?" If the buyer says yes, you are on the verge of a sale. Don't wait to go back to the office and "run some numbers"; you'll take all the wind out of the sale's sails! Ask for the order right there while the emotional levels are high.

THE TRIAL CLOSE

If you're thinking about closing, but you're not sure if it's the right time, go with a Trial Close. The Trial Close sounds like a Final Close, and it almost is. It's the last step before a Final Close, and, in fact, it must be followed by a Final Close.

Here are some sample Trial Close questions:

- "Based on everything we've discussed, does this look like the right home?"

- "Can you picture yourself pulling up to this driveway at the end of the day?"

- "Is there anything standing in your way or holding you back?"

- "Where are you in the process right now?"

- "Do you have any final questions at this time?

- "It looks like we found the right plan, the right site, the right community . . ."

Let me show you the power of this closing approach. Picture yourself asking any of the Trial Close questions listed above, and further picture a positive response from the customer. Now where are you? You are in a position where you *must* ask the Final Close question – you'll have no choice. Here is how this works in a sales office situation:

Sales Professional:	*"Is there anything standing in your way or holding you back?"*
Buyer:	*"Honestly, I can't think of anything. This looks like a really great home."*
Sales Professional:	*"Outstanding. Let's put a sold sign on it, shall we?"*

Did you hear how smoothly we went from Trial Close to Final Close? The beauty of a Trial Close is that you will have no other option but to ask for the sale. There is a very natural progression that takes place here.

Let me offer three different Trial Close approaches for you to work on. In each case I've included the progression to a brief Final Close.

- Summary Close: "Let me tell you, I work with a lot of people, and I have a good sense of when it's right and when it's not. In your case, we've found the right community, the right plan, the right homesite, the right terms.... It looks like everything works, don't you think?"

- Explain the Process: "Should you choose to purchase, let me explain how this process works from here. [Briefly explain the process from contract to close.] So that's how the process works, and the very next step would be to write a contract. Is that where you're at in the process?"

- Limited Supply: "You love this home on this homesite. And you realize there is only one homesite like this on the planet, right? Once it is gone, it is gone for good. If you know the home is right today, you should buy it today. Don't you think?"

THE FINAL CLOSE

Much of sales training focuses on the final closing questions, and these are certainly questions that you should know. However, when sales trainers focus solely on the final question and ignore the rest of the process, they are making a huge mistake. In fact, if a salesperson ignores the closing process, he probably won't be able to ask the final closing question because it's too awkward. There hasn't been a foundation laid. So for those of you who skipped the beginning of this chapter and went right to this section, go back and start at the beginning!

I subscribe to the idea that the more complex the closing attempt is the greater the likelihood is of it being screwed up! So I prefer Final Closes that are simple, natural, and conversational. Understand, though, that the Final Close questions I favor do not work in a vacuum. They are only effective when the sales counselor has been asking closing questions all throughout the process.

But think about that for a moment. If I asked all my Room Close questions, and they liked what they saw, and then I asked the Plan Close question, and they said yes, and then I walked them to a home-site and asked a Site Close question, and they said yes, where am I in this process? I am RIGHT THERE! And how sophisticated does my Final Close have to be? Not very. Frankly, if I've done everything else right, I can look at my prospect and say, "Well?" and she'll know exactly what I'm asking.

The Final Close questions are simple and natural because they are only concluding points for the closing process. These questions are critical to ask, but they should be asked naturally. Here are some sample Final Closing questions:

- "Let's put a 'sold' sign on this home, shall we?"

- "Would you like to call this your home?"

- "It'll take a few minutes to go through the paperwork. Ready?"

- "Congratulations. You're going to love this home."

- "It sounds like everything works for you. Shall we proceed?"

- "I think we've found the right home, don't you?"

- "I'm excited for you. It looks like you've found your dream home."

- "Welcome to the (Builder Name) family."

- "This is it, don't you think?"

- "Bob and Teri, this home is yours if you'd like it."

- "Let's get this started, shall we?"

Again, these questions are not scary, manipulative, or in-your-face. They are rather matter-of-fact and natural because the real work has already been done. Conversely, if you find yourself in a position where you know you're supposed to ask the final closing question, but can't, it's because you didn't ask your way into this position in the first place.

THE CLOSING CYCLE

When asking a closing question, expect a "yes," but prepare for a "no." Mediocre salespeople do not like to hear the word "no," and this can cause them to skip the closing question altogether. What a wasted opportunity. Top performers see the "no" for what it is: an opportunity!

When a customer says no, he does so because he has a lingering objection. Asking and receiving a "no" does not mean that your job is finished; it means that you need to go through the closing cycle. The closing cycle has five action steps:

1. Discover the objection.

2. Isolate the objection.

3. Overcome the objection.

4. Close on the resolution (confirm that the objection has been neutralized).

5. Ask for the sale again.

Here is a sample conversation in which the salesperson goes through the closing cycle:

Salesperson:	*"Would you like to make this home your own?"*
Customer:	*"Well, I'm not sure that it's right."*
Salesperson:	*"Fair enough. But it's clear that you like the home and the community, and this is in your desired price range. So what is holding you back?"* (1. Discover the objection)
Customer:	*"I'm still struggling with the monthly payment. It's quite a bit higher than what we were expecting."*
Salesperson:	*"Thanks for letting me know that. Is there anything else in your way, or is it just the payment issue?"* (2. Isolate the objection)
Customer:	*"No, other than that, we like the house."*
Salesperson:	*"And do you agree that you are getting quite a bit more in the home than you were planning on, what with the granite countertops, the hardwood floors, the upgraded appliance package, etc.? I can show you a home that has a payment much closer to what you were looking for, but you would have to pay extra for all those things I just mentioned or go without. I know you want the luxury of this home, and the return in resale value with these timeless upgrades is really promising."* (3. Overcome the objection)

Customer:	*"I see your point."*
Salesperson:	*In my opinion, this looks like the best overall option. Do you agree?* (4. Close on the resolution)
Customer:	*"I do."*
Salesperson:	*"You're going to love this home, and every day that you walk into it, you'll appreciate that you made the right move. Let's sit down and write up the agreement, shall we?"* (5. Ask for the sale again)

The key here is that, as a sales professional, your job is not simply to ask for the sale. Your job is to get the customer to say yes. So close, and close again, and close again!

SUMMARY

The key to closing effectively in a tough market is all about having the right mindset. Great sales professionals follow these sound principles about closing:

- "Closing is a process, not a moment in time."

- "I ask closing questions for the customer's best interest, not for my own."

- "I look for and forward to closing opportunities."

- "Closing is not something I do to my customer. It is something I do for and with my customer."

- "I am the most effective closer I can be when I incorporate closing questions as a habit in my presentation."

Get it out of your head that closing is akin to manipulation. Maybe this is the case in used car sales or in the sleaziest types of timeshare presentations, but not in new home sales. Closing is a valuable part of the service we provide our customers.

THOUGHT-PROVOKERS

1. *Do you need a mindset change on closing? Is your own yielding tendency preventing you from being the best closer you can be?*

2. *Is there one area of closing in which you are struggling? Try going back a step from that area. If you are struggling to ask the Plan Close question, work on refining your Room Close questions and see if that doesn't make the Plan Close more natural for you.*

3. *What specific Trial and Final Closes can you memorize and incorporate into your presentation this week?*

Chapter Twelve:
Selling after the Sale

Salesperson:	*"Are you ready to close in two weeks?"*
Customer:	*"We've run into a snag – a family emergency that will cost you another $10,000 in incentives if you want us to close."*
Salesperson:	*"What is it about the closing date that brings about family emergencies that all cost $10,000 that we have to pay for? Fine, I'll write the addendum."*
Customer:	*"I meant $20,000."*

"The unfinished is nothing."
Henri Frederic Amiel

Why does the mall hold such an attraction for so many people? Why do people like to bungee-jump or watch scary movies? Research by neuroscientist George Berns shows that surges in the brain of a chemical called dopamine are triggered by the *anticipation* of finding something new. Berns explains it as working this way: "You see the shoes and you get a burst of dopamine – so you buy the shoes. The anticipation is like a fuel injector for action."

This rush associated with shopping has its parallels in new home purchases. When a customer makes a decision to purchase a home, there is a corresponding dopamine rush. That "fuel injector for action" kicks in and the decision gets made. It is a wonderful reality of buying a home, and it is one of the things that give those of us in the home selling business a sense of joy.

And then it goes away. You see, the dopamine rush is associated with *anticipation.* The problem in a tough market is that negative perceptions quickly steal that joy. In other words, tough markets sap dopamine, leaving the customer in a negative mindset. So, in order to preserve the sale, the salesperson must go out of his or her way to keep the excitement going by providing emotional attachments that keep the dopamine in steady supply.

One thing I had to learn in my sales career (and it took a tough market to teach me this) was that I cannot afford to be just another negative influence that my customer experiences. I would often wear one hat before the sale: happy, gregarious, charismatic, persuasive, and exciting. But once the contract was written, I would tend to switch hats, becoming procedural in my approach: task-oriented, detailed, professorial, and analytical. Essentially, I became another source of negative input in my stressed buyers' minds.

In a strong market, this is not necessarily a concern. Customers gladly jump through hoops and stay positive because of rapid price increases. But in a tough market there is nothing to keep the customer positive if the salesperson fails to do his or her part.

Simply put, sales counselors make a mistake when they believe that the sales process is over once the contract has been signed. The truth is that the sales process must continue throughout the buying period, for several reasons:

- First, customers buy based on emotion. After they purchase, they are given a stack of very pragmatic paperwork (CCR's, disclosures, addenda, etc.) and must go through the details of loan application. The positive emotion becomes mired in the difficulties of home buying.

- Next, negative forces are at work. Be it friends, family, coworkers, or the media, everyone has an opinion on the real estate market, and these opinions are not always positive. People will "un-sell" your customer on the benefits of buying a new home.

- And then there is the dreaded "buyer's remorse." Customers will immediately ask themselves, "What have I done?" This happens as soon as the dopamine dissipates. If it happens in a strong market (and it does), imagine how challenging market conditions can exacerbate buyer's remorse.

- Finally, time works against the buyer's psyche. The longer the process stretches the more time he or she has to analyze – and overanalyze. The customer can often become exhausted in a long and often mentally grueling transaction.

Because of these factors, top performers must work throughout the buying period to counter negative emotions and messages and to assure the buyers that they have made a good decision.

Of course, selling after the sale is crucial for the salesperson's benefit as well. In a tough market, buyers will "cheat on you" after they have purchased, continuing to shop around after the contract has been written and signed. The second-guessing discussed above leads to second shopping. Offers are then made by other new home salespeople ("Cancel there and buy here. We'll give you a better deal."). Buyers in backlog are prime targets for your competitors, and to protect your sale, you must protect your buyers' energy and enthusiasm levels. You must continue to communicate to your customers that you care about them and that you are attentive to their needs. In short, you must constantly re-supply the customers with new forms of dopamine!

Selling after the sale does not just involve communication; it involves very frequent communication. Research shows that in the United States new home buyers hear from their salesperson once a month during the buying process. These same home buyers tell researchers that they would prefer to hear from the salesperson once a week. In this area, salespeople are not meeting their customers' needs.

The bottom line is that as a salesperson, you must call at least once a week, and your conversation should be a positive and upbeat *sales* message. There must be a sales purpose to every call. This is the only way to keep prospects continually excited.

Earl Robinson, VP Sales and Marketing, Baltimore, Maryland

"In a challenging market you've got to be a genuine expert on all aspects of the sale. Financing knowledge, for example, is a rare commodity in many new home sales counselors. In the old days (six months ago!) anyone could get a loan. Today sales representatives need to be better than the average loan officer on the street. My mantra: Know Thy Loan Programs!"

KEEPING A "SOLD" BUYER SOLD

Here are some strategies for selling after the sale:

1. Refresh the hot buttons. Your customer bought your home for emotional reasons. No one looks at a home in disgust and then purchases anyway. Astute sale counselors will ascertain their customers' emotional hot buttons throughout the sales process and will bring them up frequently during the transaction. These hot buttons serve to reconnect customers, and this gives them a new boost of dopamine, so talk about family, decorating, entertaining, or anything else that is emotionally charged. Be energetic and excited in your discussions.

2. Find new sales points to share. As detailed as the sales presentation might be, it is impossible for the salesperson to share everything of value about the home with the prospect before he or she purchases it. Use the buying period to continue to share nuggets of value about the home, the community, the surrounding area, the warranty, the quality of construction, etc.

3. Positively identify potential objections. The mediocre salesperson doesn't want to hear bad news, so he or she will stay away from objections. Unfortunately, objections that are not addressed lead to cancellations. During the follow-up calls the sales counselor must ask these questions directly: "Are you comfortable with the process so far? Are there any concerns that I might address? I want to make sure that you have an enjoyable experience."

4. Share good news. If interest rates come down, call the buyer. If prices go up, call the buyer. If there are three sales this week in the neighborhood, call the buyer. Plenty of bad news will reach the buyer's ears during this process; counter the bad with the good.

5. Constantly refresh your personal relationship. It is far easier to walk away from a transaction when there is no sense of commitment to an individual. In other words, canceling a contract is easier than canceling a relationship. Play up the relationship; let customers know how much you appreciate working with them, how much you are looking forward to having them live in your community, and that you think they are special.

6. Communicate much more than you think you are supposed to. After the contract has been written is absolutely the worst time to ignore the customer. Many customers are looking for a reason to cancel the transaction, and the smallest of details may set them off. If these customers are being ignored, these

details go unaddressed, and they pull the plug on the transaction. Over-communication is the order of the day; it is your hedge against surprises. For many salespeople, one phone call a week would be a significant increase in their current patterns, but this is actually the minimum amount needed to keep buyers comfortable. Especially during the end of the transaction, you'll need to consider calling them every day.

Practically speaking, here are some questions that you can use in your follow-up calls:

- "Is the process going according to your expectations?"

- "Do you have any concerns that I can help you with?"

- "Do you have any questions about the closing process?"

- "How are your moving plans coming along? Can I answer any questions about the move?"

- "Are you getting excited about your new home?"

- "When was the last time you visited your home? What did you think?"

- "Is there anything that you have been wanting to ask but forgetting about once you get near a phone?"

- "Do you have any other questions?"

AVOIDING CANCELLATIONS: TALKING BUYERS "OFF THE LEDGE"

Sometimes a sale is proceeding well when a customer calls and says, "We're having second thoughts." What caused this phone call? What are the tough-market influences that are driving your customer to cancel? The bottom line is that if the salesperson is not on top of the situation, constantly countering negatives with positives, a cancellation is a strong possibility.

When the phone call does come, you will have very little time to respond and must go into full-fledged selling mode. However, there are two very specific strategies that can be used to prevent the cancellation. First, get the customer into a logical frame of mind. One of the principles of selling is, "Get them to buy on emotion, but get them to commit on logic." In other words, emotional or fear-based cancellations are the ones that stink the most. Urge the buyer to think the situation through. Second, be prepared with specific and clear answers to the customer's logical questions. These will be unique to each customer, and so it is important to have a relationship with buyers in which you know what answers will be satisfactory to them.

To practice these strategies, think of a buyer that you have who will close in the next three to five weeks. Now come up with one positive aspect of the sale that will connect with that particular buyer. What can you tell him or her that will provide a new spurt of dopamine? (If you can't do this exercise, it's time to begin building better relationships with your customers.)

Here are the steps to managing a successful "please don't cancel" conversation:

1. Assure the customer that you are on her side. She needs to know that she has an advocate.

2. Explain that you want to help her make the right choice, whatever that may be.

3. Ask for permission to talk the situation through with her.

4. Close on an appointment. Try to have the remainder of this conversation face-to-face.

5. Lay out all the pros and cons. Make sure to come up with a long list of reasons to stay in the home. Emphasize the dominant reason that the customer chose to buy in the first place.

6. Share the facts that support moving forward.

7. Close on a decision.

8. If the buyer is still resistant, suggest a "cooling-off period." Advise her to take a couple of days to gather her thoughts.

9. Email the customer with positive reasons to stay in the deal.

SUMMARY

A great sales process is a great start, but a great start is nothing without a successful finish! Top performers make diligent and consistent efforts in communicating with their backlog at least once a week. In so doing, they keep their customers engaged and excited. They reconnect their buyers with the real reasons they purchased in the first place, and in this way they are constantly replacing the dopamine.

Service after the sale is one of the greatest gifts you can offer to your homebuyers. You've worked this hard to get the sale pointed in the right direction – don't let up now!

THOUGHT-PROVOKERS

1. *Why do you suppose that so many salespeople under-communicate with those who have already signed a contract?*

2. *Do you communicate as often as you should, and with the right purpose? Consider keeping a follow-up journal where you can track how frequently you are calling your backlog and also how effective you are in making this primarily a sales-driven call.*

Chapter Thirteen:
Finding New Business —
The Three "R's"

Salesperson: *"Is this AAA Realty? This is Wayne from ZZZ Homebuilders. Remember all those years when we summarily ignored the Realtor community? And remember when we discounted your commissions without asking you? And remember when we stopped cooperating altogether? Well, I'm just calling to let you know that we didn't really mean any disrespect, and that we really loved you the whole time, and that we know you have buyers and it would be really swell if you'd bring them over to our commun…. Hello? Hello?"*

Alex Bashenow, Sales Counselor, Indianapolis, Indiana

"In a challenging market, fundamentals must be part of the framework. Doing basics like regular Realtor contact, regular mailings to our customer base, having neighborhood functions, staying with our tasks, telling people what we are going to do, and doing what we say. Not being big talkers, but letting our performance speak for what we are doing. These things are just the ticket to the dance for us, and they always have been. If we are not willing to do these things in this market, we're out of business in a hurry."

Essentially, the single biggest difference in approach between a strong market and a tough market can come down to a salesperson's view of lead generation. In a strong market, the business comes to the salesperson. In a tough market, he or she must go out there and get it.

To find the business, salespeople should consider the "Three R's": repeat visitors, referrals, and Realtors. Of course, there are more areas besides these three that can be discussed (such as relocations, cold calling, handing out business cards, etc.), but these three primary areas bring so many opportunities that it's worthwhile to focus mainly on them. Moreover, they are areas that are often neglected by new home salespeople, and because of that there is an opportunity to really stand apart.

That said, tough markets call for creativity in reaching out to people in new and innovative ways. It is in your best interest to consider how you might find new sources of reaching potential customers.

Christine Woodcock, Owner, WRE Services, Seattle, Washington

"We must radically change what we spend our time on. Gone are the days when we could spend our time on administration, transaction management, and reports and still make a great living selling new homes. Today, we must evaluate everything we spend our time on and ask ourselves, "Is this going to help me get a sale?" If not, throw it out. Spend your time with visitors, either in person, on the phone, or through email. Spend your time doing things that are going to bring you more business or make you better prepared to sell to the next person you see."

"We most distinguish ourselves through our own marketing."
Elizabeth Gould

"Create demand."
Charles Revson

THE FIRST "R": REPEAT VISITORS

Follow-up is a separation-from-the-pack opportunity for sales professionals. Mediocre salespeople wait for business to come to them. Top professionals stay with prospects until they buy or die!

When in the market for a new home and when faced with a myriad of housing choices, the customer's first task is to eliminate options, and he will do it in one of two ways. The first way is active elimination ("I hate this house, these people, this location, etc."). The second is passive elimination ("I forgot about that neighborhood."). Follow-up after the initial visit is the salesperson's safety net against passive elimination. If the customer forgets about your community, you can consider yourself passively eliminated (and what a crime that is!). On the other hand, when done properly, follow-up is happily memorable. Follow-up will keep your community from being buried in the prospect's mind.

Every aspect of the sale is relationship-based and service-oriented, building upon a trust relationship between the customer and the salesperson. Service is the salesperson's most fundamental mission. The discipline of follow-up is no different; it should be seen as relationship-based and service-driven.

However, even if you don't land that sale through diligent follow-up effort, the practice would still be worthwhile because it separates you from the pretenders. The industry is full of pretenders to sales greatness, those who have either never learned the fundamental disciplines of sales or have abandoned them. In a tough market, these salespeople are quickly exposed.

Nowhere is a lack of fundamental discipline more evident than in follow-up. This is the first skill to be discarded or ignored when the market is strong, and it is the last to be re-adopted when the market weakens. However, in a tough market, it is an opportunity for the industrious salesperson to stand out from the crowd.

When a homebuyer visits five new home communities, how often will he be re-contacted? Statistically, he will only fill out a registration card at one of those five sales offices. That's only twenty percent of salespeople who are receiving contact information, and out of that twenty percent, less than half will actually follow up. Put simply, a potential buyer will be re-contacted less than ten percent of the time. How many wasted opportunities!

TIPS FOR EFFECTIVE FOLLOW-UP

We could dedicate an entire book to the subject of follow-up, but let's hit some of the highlights that will increase your success in this area:

1. Take useful and interesting notes. "625 FICO on a 95" is important information, but it's not all that interesting. "Job relo from L.A.; needs to move within 90 days; two kids in grade school; wife (Janet) works for United Airlines; looking for two home offices or one big office; likes plan 4 (especially kitchen); showed lot 16 and 23." That's interesting and useful information. It will pay off when it's time to make the follow-up call.

2. Promise to call while the customer is still in your office. Get the permission to call while the customer is still around. Try saying, "I'll call you later this week to let you know about X," or, "I'll call you on Monday to see how you liked community Y." Not only does the customer now expect your call, but because your integrity is at stake, you are most likely to go through with the follow-up.

3. Determine the follow-up strategy right after the customer leaves the office. The wrong time to determine strategy is when you are staring at the registration card trying to determine why you should call back. Instead, the moment the customer leaves the sales office, flip over the registration card and write

the next step. For example, "Call on Monday with costs for room change," or, "Call tomorrow to close the sale." Be sure to also write the time and date for the follow-up call in your appointment book.

4. Call back within one day if the buyer is an "A" prospect, two days if he or she is a "B" prospect, and three days if he or she is a "C" prospect. In fact, for "A" prospects there is no reason to wait even twenty-four hours – call them later the same day!

5. Mail a thank-you card within one day of the initial visit. A handwritten note is preferred, especially for "A" prospects. Remember to include some of the personal information you've gathered ("I hope Brittany won her soccer game!").

6. Continue to call "A" prospects until they buy or die. If you are worried about bugging them, remember that you've got nothing to lose! By closing often through follow-up, you can eventually be more direct in your approach. For example, "Look, you've been thinking about this for weeks, and the only thing that is happening is that the best locations are continuing to sell. It's time to make a decision before someone else buys the homesite that you have already selected. Are you ready to make that decision right now?"

7. Smile before you dial. The customer can actually hear the expression on your face – it comes across in your tone.

8. Set a follow-up goal. Set aside thirty minutes of uninterrupted time to make the calls, and don't do anything else (you'll need to do this before or after office hours). Or take a stack of fifteen registration cards and vow not to get out of your chair until all the calls have been made. Once you've completed a call, immediately make the next call. Don't get coffee; don't check e-mails; just keep pounding away until you've reached your mini-goal.

Try this activity to practice the discipline of follow-up. Read the following scenario and make the follow-up call.

Scenario: The customers liked Plan One and walked to three homesites with you; they liked lot 33 the best. You attempted the "Explain the Process" close (they are first-time buyers). He replied that part of the down payment is coming from his annual bonus and he must confirm with his boss that the bonus is in fact on the way. The couple told you during the visit that they were going to see a movie later in the evening.

How would that call go? What's the first thing out of your mouth? What would you talk about first? What energy would you need to have? What is the goal of the call?

THE SECOND "R": REFERRALS

Referrals from existing homebuyers or past visitors are always beneficial, but in a tough market, they are critically important. A tough market is characterized by buyer fear. Prospective buyers fear market conditions, the media, and making a bad decision. However, when a person buys a home, he or she is exhibiting belief in the market; consequently, these people are your best allies. They have already been "converted"; they have already been through the process of justifying their purchase, both to themselves and others. They are the most convinced believers in the market, and that makes them good salespeople!

When prospects come into the sales office as referrals, they are real buyers, not lookers. These customers know the issues and concerns and have heard the bad news. However, knowing that there are other choices, they are still standing in *your* office! What about these prospects looks anything less than A-plus?!

Salespeople with a strong yielding tendency can tend to struggle in asking for referrals. They fear this possibility of rejection, just as they fear all rejection. However, the benefits of referrals far outweigh the possibility of rejection. The successful salesperson will imply that referrals are expected. Furthermore, she will let buyers know that referrals work in their own best interests. More sales bring a quicker end to construction in the area, allow buyers to select their own neighbors, and increase property values.

Remember as well that salespeople are not limited only to homebuying customers as potential referrals. Great sales counselors provide excellent service to every single visitor. Even if the visitor does not purchase, the salesperson has still earned the right to ask for referrals.

Ask for referrals directly and without apology. Consider the following referral request:

"I'm thrilled that you've chosen this community to live in and that you've chosen our company to build your new home. Now you have the opportunity to select your neighbors. Is there anyone you can think of that would also consider living in this neighborhood?"

Simple, natural, effective. Try it in your own sales process. Set a referral goal and stick by it.

THE THIRD "R": REALTORS

The final "R" is for the Realtors, whose cooperation becomes invaluable in a tough market. You cannot deny it – Realtors have buyer leads that you want at your community.

However, effective Realtor promotions are primarily about relationships, not special programs. While special Realtor events can help, this is not the preferred method for reaching out to the Realtor community. The problem is that the time to start building a Realtor base was five years ago. In a tough market, Realtors are being courted by every new home sales representative in town, and it will be difficult to get their attention. Cultivating these relationships takes time, and salespeople must understand the importance of building long-term partnerships with Realtors.

Here are a few starting points for fostering such partnerships:

- Give the Realtors the VIP treatment. Realtors are often leery of new home sales professionals, so you need to go out of your way to compliment their success. It's okay to gush.

- Alleviate the Realtor's fears. Realtors can be a paranoid sort. After all, when they lose their clients, they lose the commission that goes along with that buyer. Their clients are their only source of income. You, on the other hand, can always sell to the next person to come through the door. To ease this fear, let the Realtor know right from the beginning that your business relationship is a partnership. Tell him that you will not destroy the trust he has developed with his client and that your job is to make him look good.

- Make the Realtor's life easy. Promise extra services at no charge. Tell her to feel free to come by the office for cold water, to use the fax machine, or to make a phone call whenever she's in the area. Offer her the use of your model to write a contract with a customer. Bend over backwards.

- Make the Realtor look good in front of the prospect. Realtors are constantly trying to impress their clients, and you can help. Go out of your way to comment on the Realtor's professionalism and/or knowledge.

- Stay in touch. You should be constantly communicating with a stable of at least ten productive Realtors. Many successful new home salespeople regularly communicate with twenty-five or more Realtors through weekly phone calls (not just email blasts). To effectively build a Realtor base, build the relationships so that you are on a first-name basis. This requires constant phone calls and emails, alerting them to exceptionally good deals. Go out of your way to make them feel like VIP's. Your goal is to have Realtors think of you first.

DEFENDING YOUR VALUE WITH REALTORS

One issue that needs to be addressed here is incentives, especially when a Realtor asks for your incentives over the phone ("I'm not bringing my prospect out until you tell me your best deal."). Don't yield and don't answer. The Realtors with which you have long-term relationships already know your incentives, so you don't have to worry about that.

The Realtors who call demanding incentives are deal-driven, not customer-driven. If they are comparison shopping on the phone, you can't win unless you have the highest incentive. It doesn't matter if you have the best home for the customer; if you don't have the highest incentive, you are immediately eliminated. There is no good reason to answer the incentive question to a Realtor over the phone.

Try this response instead: "Let me turn the tables. If it were your listing and I had the buyer, and I called and asked you to reveal to me the lowest price your seller would be willing to take before I even bring my prospect out, let alone make an offer, would you disclose that private information? Of course not. You have a fiduciary responsibility to your seller not to. I'm in the same position. When your customer wants to write a contract on the home he loves, then we'll talk incentives."

You also need to look at defending value during the demonstration. You don't want the Realtor offering negative comments about your offering, so enlist the customer's help in avoiding that discomfort. Do this by asking the customer a closing question ("Does this kitchen work for you?"). When the customer responds positively, immediately turn to the Realtor and ask the same question ("And what do you think – does this meet their needs?"). If the Realtor chooses to take a swipe at your product, he now has to negate your customer's sense of value in order to do so.

SUMMARY

It's simple, really. If the market changes a little, you must change your approach a little. But if the market changes a lot, you must change your approach A LOT! Too many salespeople are infected with a sense of entitlement ("The business will come to me."). That mindset will get you clobbered in a tough market.

While there are many types of outreach available to new home sales counselors, the "Big Three" are Repeat Visitors, Referrals, and Realtors.

THOUGHT-PROVOKERS

1. *What areas of outreach have you neglected? What is your immediate action item based on this discussion?*

2. *What is holding you back in this area? What aspect of your mental game do you need to work on to be the best you can be?*

3. *What outreach opportunities can you consider that are outside of the "Three R's"? What unique opportunities do you have to reach more prospects?*

Postscript

*"Those who do not read
are no better off than those who cannot read."*
Mark Twain

Congratulations, you made it to the end! Or, perhaps, to the beginning, depending on how you wish to look at things. Re-read the quote by Mark Twain at the top of this page. Now let me amend that quote just a bit:

*Those who do not use the tools they are given
are no better off than those who were never given the tools
in the first place.*

This is my fear: that you put this book on the shelf saying, "Yeah, there was some good stuff in there," but then you never apply what you have learned. That, to me, would be tragic, and it would negate our collective hours spent – me writing and you reading this book.

I beg you not to let that happen. Growth is so critical to your success because there is no such thing as stagnation. You are getting better, or you are getting worse. And when you stop getting better, you start getting worse. Period.

The greatest service you can offer your customers in a challenging market is to serve them to your highest potential, and this comes through your dedication to constant improvement. Let me urge you to action, each and every day of your life.

Finally, when the market is challenging and the traffic is down, when you get hit with a couple of unexpected cancellations and the boss snipes at you, when Realtors malign your price point, or when the media runs yet another doom-saying lead story, stop and remember that you cannot control your circumstances, but you can always control your response to your circumstances. In other words, no one has the power to make you feel bad without your permission. *You* control your own emotions, and *you* control your own state of mind. Pain is inevitable; misery is a choice.

Howard Flaschen, Sales Counselor, Jacksonville, Florida

"In creating optimism in this tough environment, I focus on the fun that this job can be. When you get the opportunity to open that door for someone, you truly get to have a ball with them. Your buyers will remember their time with you more than anyone else they've seen all day. I actually had one customer buy a home because she said that after seeing numerous homes and having them all blend together, she remembered the "Howard house" where I laid down in front of the fireplace! I had a ball, she had a ball, and she bought from me because we had a ball. In a day that wants to smother you in the negative, push you down, and fill you with rejection, you have to find those spots, take advantage of those moments, and make sure that you are having a ball because when you're having fun, they're having fun, and there is no doubt that a buyer is more apt to buy from you when they like you than when they don't. Heck, if they don't buy from you today at least you got to smile, make them smile, and you had a great time with them . . . they'll remember you. I promise."

And in those tough days, think of the words of the late Dave Stone:

> *"Selling new homes and new home communities is one of*
> *the most complex and, at the same time, one of the most*
> *exciting professions in the world. If you can accept the*
> *roles you play and the challenges you receive, you may well*
> *discover that, unlike many who go through life without*
> *any great sense of achievement, you will be able to look*
> *back on your life in later years and say, 'You know what;*
> *I was pretty good. I helped a lot of people to own homes.*
> *I have molded a lot of lives. I influenced one of the most*
> *important things in the world – the way people live.'"*

Hope you've enjoyed the book, and may God bless you each and every day.

Now go change someone's world!

About the Author

Jeff Shore is a contemporary expert in the area of new home sales and sales management, and the industry authority on selling in a tough market.

The former National Sales Director for KBHome, Jeff is a student of sales first and a teacher second. His leadership is far from theoretical – Jeff started his new home career as a sales representative in Northern California where he sold in excess of 500 homes (in extremely difficult market conditions!). He moved up to Vice President of Sales and Marketing for a 1,000+ unit homebuilding division. He went on to his corporate position where he wrote and delivered training programs, coached managers and directed sales strategy. Jeff has been training independently since 1999.

Today, Shore Consulting provides strategy and training services to homebuilding companies large and small across the country.

Jeff Shore resides in Auburn, California with his wife and best friend, Karen.

For more information about booking Jeff Shore to work with your organization, to find out about upcoming seminars in your area, or to purchase multiple copies of *Tough Market New Home Sales*, please visit:

www.JeffShore.com

CPSIA information can be obtained
at www.ICGtesting.com
Printed in the USA
FSOW02n0412280116
16193FS